# BLACK PANTHER

## 21ˢᵀ CENTURY FILM ESSENTIALS

Cinema has a storied history, but its story is far from over. *21ˢᵗ Century Film Essentials* offers a lively chronicle of cinema's second century, examining the landmark films of our ever-changing moment. Each book makes a case for the importance of a particular contemporary film for artistic, historical, or commercial reasons. The twenty-first century has already been a time of tremendous change in filmmaking the world over, from the rise of digital production and the ascent of the multinational blockbuster to increased vitality in independent filmmaking and the emergence of new voices and talents both on screen and off. The films examined here are the ones that embody and exemplify these changes, crystallizing emerging trends or pointing in new directions. At the same time, they are films that are informed by and help refigure the cinematic legacy of the previous century, showing how film's past is constantly reimagined and rewritten by its present. These are films both familiar and obscure, foreign and domestic; they are new but of lasting value. This series is a study of film history in the making. It is meant to provide a different kind of approach to cinema's story—one written in the present tense.

Donna Kornhaber, Series Editor

## Also in the series

J. J. Murphy, *The Florida Project*
Patrick Keating, *Harry Potter and the Prisoner of Azkaban*
Dana Polan, *The LEGO Movie*

# Black Panther

## Scott Bukatman

UNIVERSITY OF TEXAS PRESS ❖ AUSTIN

Requests for permission to reproduce material from
this work should be sent to:
    Permissions
    University of Texas Press
    P.O. Box 7819
    Austin, TX 78713-7819
    utpress.utexas.edu/rp-form

♾ The paper used in this book meets the minimum requirements
of ANSI/NISO Z39.48-1992 (R1997) (Permanence of Paper).

Library of Congress Cataloging-in-Publication Data

Names: Bukatman, Scott, 1957– author.
Title: Black Panther / Scott Bukatman.
Other titles: 21st century film essentials.
Description: First edition. | Austin : University of Texas Press, 2022. |
    Series: 21st century film essentials | Includes index.
Identifiers: LCCN 2021047901
    ISBN 978-1-4773-2584-1 (cloth)
    ISBN 978-1-4773-2535-3 (paperback)
    ISBN 978-1-4773-2536-0 (PDF)
    ISBN 978-1-4773-2537-7 (ePub)
Subjects: LCSH: Black Panther (Motion picture : 2018) | Black Panther
    (Fictitious character)—In motion pictures. | Coogler, Ryan,
    1986—Criticism and interpretation. | Black Panther (Motion picture :
    2018)—Political aspects. | Black Panther (Motion picture : 2018)—Social
    aspects. | Black Panther (Motion picture : 2018)—Influence. | Wakanda
    (Africa : Imaginary place) | Superheroes, Black. | African diaspora in
    art. | Afrofuturism. | Women, Black, in motion pictures. | Fantasy
    films—Political aspects—United States.
Classification: LCC PN1997.2.B5815 B85 2022 | DDC 791.43/72—dc23/
    eng/20211027
LC record available at https://lccn.loc.gov/2021047901

doi:10.7560/325353

I didn't know how much I wanted a dog before Iggy, a kid before Linus, or a partner before Beth.

This book is for them.

# Contents

BLACK PANTHER

# Preface

Turns out, I *seriously* underestimated the power of the superhero.

My writing has, for decades now, celebrated the liberatory fantasy of superheroes. I've long been drawn to the alternative bodies that popular media provides in such abundance, be they in cartoons, musicals, Jerry Lewis movies, or the world of superheroes. Sergei Eisenstein found in the unruly animated bodies of early Walt Disney cartoons a "freedom from once and forever allotted form," and, at its best, the superhero offers something similar.[1] Where so many others (including, briefly, myself) found in superhero comics little more than white masculinist power fantasies, I found mutability, fluidity of identity, and a rich corporeal imagination. Where others emphasized the traumatic underpinnings of many a superhero as proof of the genre's seriousness, I sought out playfulness and flamboyant performance. And while the genre "grew up" in a thousand ways, from the ambitions of its writers and the sophistication of its artists to its increasing engagement with the real world, I (and I wasn't alone) cautioned that we shouldn't forget the naivete and silliness of its origins.

But in elaborating upon the rich corporeal utopia of the superhero, I failed to acknowledge that it was a fantasy more accessible for some than others. Superheroes were, for me, race and gender neutral, allegorically queer, and generically human.

They just happened to be mostly white and male. That didn't exclude marginalized or minoritarian readers or viewers from engaging with superheroic fantasy, but what I didn't get was that a different and far less utopian meaning arose in the fissures between white male (super) powers and peoples whose relation to power in any of its manifestations was constrained. White bodies, after all, *already* exist within and act upon the world with a relative dearth of inhibitions and restraints.

My (*ahem*) major writings on superheroes appeared before their astonishing re-emergence as a mass popular form. Superheroes once belonged to *me*,[2] and now they were a major area of entertainment and academic study; did I resent their new prominence? But my resistance to the superhero movie, immortalized in my 2011 essay "Why I Hate Superhero Movies," began to wane. The year 2018 was a kind of annus mirabilis for the genre, what with *Teen Titans GO! To the Movies* (Peter Rida Michail and Aaron Horvath), *Spider-Man: Into the Spider-Verse* (Bob Persichetti, Peter Ramsey, and Rodney Rothman), *Ant-Man and the Wasp* (Peyton Reed), and, of course, *Black Panther* (Ryan Coogler). *Captain Marvel* (Anna Boden and Ryan Fleck) followed in 2019.[3]

I've often said that some movies needn't be good to be great—their impact on culture, or on the medium itself, might outweigh their objective "quality." *Tron* (Steven Lisberger, 1982) is such a movie, its cyberspatial imagination vastly more interesting than its corporate espionage plot or the flatness of its characters. *Black Panther* might well have been another: the first movie to feature a major Black superhero and the first superhero franchise movie directed by an African American— not to mention the highest grossing movie *ever* by an African American director. Audiences greeted it rapturously, thrilled

to see a superhero that, as the saying goes, "looked like them."
Its "essential" place in history was assured.

But *Black Panther* is both great *and* good: a remarkably
warm, even loving, movie with spectacular world-building; a
hero-villain conflict structured around ideas of Black liberation and social responsibility; strong women characters in
varied roles; all the myriad pleasures of color, music, costume,
and fight choreography; and sensational performances from
gorgeous actors. I jumped at the chance to write a short book
about it, figuring it to be a kind of culmination of my thinking
about superheroes and a sign of my conversion to the possibilities of this cinematic genre. I might need some remedial education in critical race theory, I flippantly thought, but otherwise,
hey, I had this covered.[4]

Then the world overtook me, and it changed *Black Panther*.
There was the pandemic, which made racial imbalances in
America stunningly visible. Stunningly visible, too, was the
murder of George Floyd, captured for the world to see, and
the other deaths that sparked an upsurgence in the Black Lives
Matter movement and a plunge into a recognition of the systemic racism permeating American institutions, including my
own home of academia. Finally, the death of Chadwick Boseman revealed once more the centrality of *Black Panther* to the
Black community, but where the movie's release had been the
occasion for joyous celebration, Boseman's death was another
blow to a community that had already, in 2020, suffered so
much.

*Black Panther* became an "Important" movie, one that
surely deserved more than my usual ruminations on fun fantasies of flying bodies. Race could no longer be just one element
among others to explore; now it needed to be at the center.

That I, a white scholar, should be the person tasked with writing about this movie at this time, was a Thing I needed to consider and reconsider. My writing has always been filtered through my own experience, but this called for something both more expansive and more specific. No longer could I generically refer to "our" bodies and experiences when bodily experiences that were explicitly and urgently *not* mine were the topic at hand. The complications of language loomed: I couldn't use "we" but could hardly say "they." As I considered other forms of difference, I realized the phrase "differently abled" seemed ridiculous when the subject was superheroes. Which words to capitalize became a major debate as I was writing (does capitalizing "White" denaturalize the term or align it with supremacy?). I had to decide whether what you're reading now should be a preface or an afterword. And there wasn't a single good term that could encompass bodies of different shades, sizes, genders, or sexual orientations. Then there was the time my spell checker turned "Black interiority" into "Black inferiority." I soldiered on.

I began to feel the weight of it all. And weight, as my friends and students well know, is not my thing. It didn't help that I was researching and reading and writing in what I came to think of as "pandemic style"—writing something, *anything*, whenever I could grab some time. I didn't enjoy writing in a pandemic vacuum. I *was* excited by the scholarship I was engaging, which helped me find different ways of theorizing specifically Black (or Other) superheroes—including ways that moved beyond overt politics and ideas of abjection—and I took some satisfaction in working outside my comfort zone. But the task of putting it all together forced me to realize that my book about this deeply fun movie had become no fun.

There was some good news: my earlier work on the liberating corporeal imagination of the superhero was hardly irrelevant to the consideration of a Black cinematic superhero—it was a necessary premise upon which a more specific and trenchant analysis could be built. Race obviously mattered in superhero stuff in ways I hadn't thought enough about. It's all well and good to present a superhero like the green-skinned Brainiac 5 as an allegorical avatar of racial difference, but metaphorical engagements that elide specific histories of race won't go far in redressing large-scale cultural erasures.[5]

A watershed moment in the history of racial representation in the world of superheroes was the opening scene of *Green Lantern* #76 (April 1970, written by Denny O'Neil and penciled by Neal Adams)—the first issue in which the character was teamed with a streetwise Green Arrow.[6] It begins with Green Lantern rescuing a white man from an angry Black crowd, only to be informed by Green Arrow that he's just "saved" a slumlord from his justifiably irate tenants. Up shuffles an elderly Black man, who delivers a now iconic monologue:

> I been readin' about you.... How you work for the **blue skins**... and how on a planet someplace you helped out the **orange skins** ... and you done considerable for the **purple skins**! Only there's **skins** you never bothered with—the **black** skins! I want to know... **how come**?! Answer me **that**, Mr. **Green Lantern**!

A deeply chagrined Mr. Green Lantern answers, "I ... *can't*."[7]

In the years since, there were those in the fan community who pointed out that Green Lantern, in saving the world

innumerable times, had done "considerable" for the "black skins,"
which kind of missed the point (the superhero equivalent of
"All lives matter"). Not unlike those clueless fans, though, I had
failed to consider the impact of superheroes who more literally
embodied disenfranchised or marginalized races and cultures,
who could—in their very being—articulate new relations of
power and assertions of being. All the kids who dressed in
tribal or superhero regalia to go see *Black Panther* (the movie
*and* the hero) revealed just how singular, how monumental,
and how utopian an *event* this movie proved to be. But focusing on the cute kids ran the risk of overlooking how *Black
Panther* spoke more deeply to *adults* of color, whose historical
awareness and experience with navigating the world "while
Black" could encourage even more intense responses to the
utopian alternatives displayed on screen.

The greater visibility and cost of blockbuster movies, not
to mention the global market, has been a major factor driving Marvel and DC to diversify their superheroes and not just
their sidekicks—so, you know, good. Cinema's phenomenological power moves beyond representation and signification to
a more direct experience of presence. For women, people of
color(s), and those from marginalized cultures, there are high
stakes in these heroes made flesh—*incarnated*, *embodied*, *powered*, and *hyper-visible* (visible not only within the narrative
but in the cultural world of the audience). The on-screen superhero has proven so compelling to so many that audiences
have practically demanded a roster of heroes diverse in ways
that move beyond the color of the energy beams shooting from
their fingers; they have waited with increasingly less patience
for heroes who look like them.

Superheroes embodying cultural differences had all the

resonances I'd found in superheroes generally, and a whole lot more. They present utopian (which doesn't mean naive) alternatives for groups whose visibility in the world falls to the margins, whose ability to act upon the world is always already constrained, whose willfullness is often misread as threat. Writer upon writer has considered the ways that Black people and women are defined from the outside by a controlling and defining gaze—individual and institutionalized—that is white or male or both, a gaze that positions them as objects rather than subjects. To systematically constrain someone's ability to act, or to just be, becomes, at some point, a constraint upon their ability to dream.

All of this makes the movie *great*, but what about the things that make it not just good, but *so* good? I'd forgotten another of my guiding truths: movies don't need to be *serious* to be great. *Black Panther* indeed deals in weighty issues, and the profundity of the Black bodies at its center rewards the deepest scrutiny. But it's also exuberant and richly imagined, and it has a most excellent car chase—of which my son was *very* enamored but which I hadn't even *mentioned*—with Okoye riding shotgun (or spear, whichever works) while Shuri whoops it up, virtually piloting her car from half a world away. Oh, and there's the Afrofuturist and Pan-African beauty of the mythical African nation of Wakanda. *Black Panther* bursts with the good feeling that comes from movies that respect—even love—their characters, to say nothing of their audience. I've been watching and watching it, and I have yet to tire of it—even as it became a more bittersweet experience with the loss of Chadwick Boseman.

*Black Panther* is a true crossover success—a work of Black popular culture emanating from within the Disney/Marvel behemoth, one that succeeded with superhero nerds and newbies alike. It was a movie conceived in Obama's America but released in Trump's, where it was much needed. It demonstrates the continuing power of popular culture to articulate utopian ideals and raise questions that it may not (or can not) fully resolve. *Black Panther* is a vehicle for utopian dreaming in myriad ways both race-specific and more broadly humanist. No small thing.

*Black Panther* carried meanings for its Black audiences that I didn't recognize. But I've learned. And along the way, I've come to realize that perhaps this movie didn't "need" me the way the subjects of some of my other writings have needed me—*Black Panther* was going to be written about with or without me. Rather, *I* needed *Black Panther* to help me think differently about the world.

I'm honored to have had the opportunity to write this book about this movie. It's not meant to be the last word (or the last book) on *Black Panther*. There's so much more to be written, and I can't wait to read it.

Like I said, I seriously underestimated the power of the superhero.

# Introduction

# Tell Me a Story

"Tell me a story."

*Black Panther* begins—*begins* begins, even before the Marvel Studios logo—with a black screen, and the voice of a boy imploring his father to tell him a story. "Which one?" asks the father. "The story of home," comes the answer. The movie, then, a big-budget, digital-effects-laden blockbuster from Marvel Studios, a subsidiary of the Disney Corporation, immediately asserts itself as a kind of folklore.[1]

The accents mark the boy as American; the father, African. Upon re-viewing we will realize that the father is N'Jobu, younger brother of T'Chaka (father of T'Challa, who will, upon his father's demise, assume the mantle of Black Panther), and his son is Erik, who will grow to become Killmonger, the Panther's formidable and tragic nemesis. Erik, the American boy, is asking for the story of Wakanda, which this African father, and this prologue, will proceed to tell:

Millions of years ago, a meteorite made of vibranium, the strongest substance in the universe, struck the continent of Africa, affecting the plant life around it. And when the time of man came, five tribes settled on it and called

it Wakanda. The tribes lived in constant war with each
other until a warrior shaman received a vision from the
Panther goddess Bast, who led him to the heart-shaped
herb, a plant that granted him superhuman strength,
speed, and instincts. The warrior became king and the
first Black Panther, the protector of Wakanda.

*The first Black Panther.*

These words are illustrated by digital animation of shifting, sinuous sands in a limited palette of blacks and browns,
punctuated by the piercing blue of vibranium and the purple
associated with the herb. Figures emerge and sublimate: some
literal (the meteor striking Earth), others allegorical (five fists,
for the five tribes, appear and clasp one another). The camera
elegantly weaves through these incessantly morphing shapes—
an effect even more marvelous in 3D.

"The Wakandans used vibranium to develop technology
more advanced than any other nation"—a modern city rises
from the sand—"but as Wakanda thrived the world around it
descended further into chaos." The sand forms images: cen-
turion combat, chained Africans loaded onto ships, the tanks

and planes of World War II. "To keep vibranium safe, the Wakandans vowed to hide in plain sight, keeping the truth of their power from the outside world." A shimmering blue veil covers the city in an illusion of uninhabited forest.

The prologue has the practical virtue of filling in the Wakandan backstory (also a good reason to quote it here); it was added after test screenings indicated some confusion in those less steeped in the world of Marvel superheroes. But it's more resonant than that. To begin with a child asking for a story is to link the story of *Black Panther* (and perhaps superheroes in general) to the world of childhood. It also evokes oral traditions of transmitting knowledge and culture that predate cultures of writing and print—hence the appropriateness of "writing" this story in shifting sands, whether digital or not.

*Black Panther* is offered to us as both mythic lore and Marvel lore (which for some of us is nearly the same thing)—an entwining of mass and folk cultures.

Perhaps most poignantly, it's the voice of an American child asking his elder for a story about Africa, about *home*. Asking for stories that may or may not be written, but which are surely seldom taught. Their final interchange is crucial to the plot that will now unfold, but it also speaks more broadly to an African American child's awakening political consciousness.

"And we still hide, Baba?"

"Yes."

*"Why?"*

*Black Panther* tells the story of the new king, T'Challa (Chadwick Boseman), who is also, through the magic of the "heart-shaped herb," the superpowered Black Panther. It tells of the king's confrontation with his half-Wakandan cousin

Erik "Killmonger" Stevens (Michael B. Jordan), a child whom King T'Chaka abandoned to the streets of Oakland after killing N'Jobu, his father, for selling vibranium, and who has returned to claim his birthright.

The film also stages a sustained debate around the responsibility of Wakanda to the rest of the world—the transformative potential of its technology and weaponry to liberate oppressed Black peoples. N'Jobu pleads with T'Chaka: "Their leaders have been assassinated, communities flooded with drugs and weapons. They are overly policed and incarcerated. All over the planet our people suffer because they don't have the tools to fight back." Killmonger's plan is just this: to provide Wakandan weapons to outside struggles. Though Killmonger is ultimately defeated, the film tells of T'Challa's growing sense that Wakanda has a greater responsibility to the world—and the world's oppressed—than it has heretofore honored.

This book is the story of those stories in this movie, but there are yet more stories to tell.

There's the history (and prehistory) of superheroes in comics—the ground from which *Black Panther* emerges. The extraordinary body of the superhero—across media—has incarnated dreams and fears and allegories of all kinds; it's a fiercely, *insistently* embodied genre that's richer and more nuanced than even many of its fans might think.

There's the history of Marvel superhero comics: in the 1960s, Marvel introduced more complex psychologies and a more profound sense of trauma, with heroes who were often tormented by their powers or tormented for having them. Marvel introduced an archness of tone that acknowledged the (let's admit it) fundamental absurdity of the genre. It innovated in serial storytelling, introducing stories that reached across multiple issues and characters that crossed over into one another's adventures. Marvel comics attracted an older audience, notably on college campuses. A remarkable number of characters that debuted in the efflorescence of 1961–1966 are still in circulation, including Black Panther.

There's the history of non-white and non-male superheroes on page and screen—their move from erasure, to the margins, to superstardom.

This is also the story of Black Panther, the first Black superhero offered up by mainstream comics: from his introduction in the pages of *Fantastic Four* in 1966 through his recent incarnations in comics scripted by Ta-Nehisi Coates and the blockbuster movie.[2] And it's the story of the Panther's passage from the hands of two Jewish American creators, Jack Kirby and Stan Lee, to those of other writers and artists, among them African American writers Christopher Priest and Reginald Hudlin, and artists Billy Graham, Denys Cowan, and Brian Stelfreeze. Early on, Wakanda's development as a culture and society was mapped by white writer Don McGregor in the pages of *Jungle Action* comics, and the equally white Roy Thomas chronicled the Panther's life as an Avenger. These legacies, these histories, and this lore are all part of *Black Panther*.

There's the story of Wakanda—that other, equally radical creation of the Lee-Kirby team. Introduced as a high-tech jungle whose sophistication staggers even the genius of Reed Richards of the Fantastic Four, it's an African nation with nothing of the "primitive" about it, an African nation never conquered, never colonized, never subservient. Small wonder Wakanda was foundational to the ethos and aesthetic later labeled Afrofuturist; small wonder so much of *Black Panther* takes place within its borders.

Yet another story is of the transmediality of the superhero, a figure that emerged in nascent forms from pulp magazines before soaring in to comic books and soaring out to radio, animation, movies, television, and games. Until the twenty-first century, nearly all superhero media production was geared toward the young; just a few iterations bothered with adults.

And so there is the story of the Marvel Cinematic Universe. Marvel failed for decades to realize the value of its own intellectual property—until it did. Kevin Feige's plan to release a slate of movies that interconnected, like the comics that preceded them, was successful beyond anyone's imagining, spearheading, for good and ill, a popular culture juggernaut that shows no signs of weakening while making household names of Iron Man, Green Lantern, Ant-Man, Thor, and, yes, Black Panther. The cinematic incarnation of the Panther appeared first in *Captain America: Civil War* (Anthony and Joe Russo, 2016) and was featured in the culminating Avengers movies of the MCU's first decade, *Infinity War* (Anthony and Joe Russo, 2018) and *Endgame* (Anthony and Joe Russo, 2019). DC Comics, of course, had a universe of its own to bring to synergistic life; superheroes from both universes took up prominent positions on television as well as in movies.

The accelerating move toward greater diversity in the world of superhero media, too, is a story. The global appeal of the movies demanded greater inclusivity, which eventually brought Wonder Woman, Black Lightning, Captain Marvel, and Black Panther to screens large and small, along with such racially diverse teams as the X-Men and (Teen) Titans. These characters came from comics, but I'd suggest that the vastly greater audience for film and television goaded comics publishers toward a more diverse roll call of heroes, yielding, to take but two examples, Kamala Khan, a Muslim American Ms. Marvel, and Miles Morales, an Afro-Latino Spider-Man. There's also the way that *Black Panther* made women—as spies, soldiers, scientists, warriors, and council elders—as central as its titular male superhero.

There is the story of a superhero movie becoming the highest grossing film by a Black director, and how Ryan Coogler infused this corporate-franchise blockbuster with his own tone, his own concerns, and, crucially, his own crew and casting preferences. And there is the story of the making of the film, with its dazzling visual imagination, powerful performances, and indelible characters. And the story of *Black Panther*'s popular and critical reception, and the continuing debates around its ideological import and valence.

It's the story of the Black audiences who felt a yearning for the movie's idealized but poignant African imaginary, for a land neither conquered nor riven. And there is the story of the loss of Chadwick Boseman, a trauma that topped off a year of traumas. Children staged mock funerals; parents struggled with how to tell them the news.[3]

The story the son requests at the start is "the story of home"—he means Wakanda, but one could think of *Black Panther* presenting itself as a kind of home, a welcoming haven, and, yes, a utopia, for all of us but especially for those Black children who could finally see a superhero movie in which the heroes were like them.

*Black Panther* is a terrific movie, though by itself that's not quite enough to justify its inclusion in the 21st Century Film Essentials series. It could certainly be considered essential as an example of some key twenty-first-century American moviemaking and marketing practices—as a franchise block-buster and superhero movie—but other movies (including some in this series) could check some of those boxes. But as the most successful American movie directed by someone who isn't a white male, a movie with an almost exclusively Black cast, a movie that was, moreover, (to use Carvell Wallace's lovely phrase) "steeped . . . in blackness," *Black Panther* stands as a singular work.[4] I'll let you in on a secret: the editor of this series, Donna Kornhaber, had *Panther* in mind when she conceived the series in the first place.

Whatever unconscious biases I may have (and I'm sure they're legion), I have a couple of *conscious* biases to confirm at the outset. I'm not oblivious to *Black Panther*'s status as part of a series that constitutes the Marvel Cinematic Universe, but, for me, the "essential" nature of the movie comes—mostly—through its status as a discrete aesthetic experience. Nobody experiences art in a vacuum; we can't help but bring ourselves, with our particular histories, to our engagement with art, which allows us to engage with it dialogically. *Black Panther* will resonate differently for (to be stereotypical about it) a white Marvel nerd than for (another stereotype) an older African American woman with little detailed knowledge of the history of, say, Ultron's relation to Wonder Man or who that guy was in the last post-credit scene. Black viewers might see the movie differently from white ones (and different Black viewers will experience the movie differently from each other). Those seeing it on a large screen may have a different experience from that of a home viewer—and so on. Different though the viewing experiences may be, they all involve the discrete work called *Black Panther*, which will be the main focus of this book. That's not to deny the specific ways the movie resonates as one installment of a larger, ongoing, transmedial "work," and I promise to consider that in its turn. But *Black Panther* just does not feel like other superhero movies; like the very different *Logan* (James Mangold, 2017), it builds its own cinematic world, with its own tone and its own set of references.[5]

My other bias: I'm an unabashed auteurist who (mostly) appreciates art as some*thing* some*one* made. *Black Panther* is a product of the Disney Corporation, which now owns Marvel Studios, and is the product of the labor of hundreds of artists, artisans, technicians, and executive types. All of that's important, but it's also a movie by Ryan Coogler, and his fingerprints are all over it. That's a context I choose to accentuate, while still acknowledging the other voices in play.[6]

The first chapter sets out some of the ideas and history leading to *Black Panther*, followed by three longer explorations of central aspects of the movie: the corporeality of Black Panther and of Black superheroes (or those from other underrepresented groups) more generally; the complexities of Wakanda as myth, historical entity, feminist stronghold, and Pan-African fantasy; and the way the movie's rhetorical strategies complicate our relation to its ostensible villain, Killmonger.

# The Road to Wakanda

Getting to *Black Panther* involves a number of histories—of superhero comics; of Marvel; of the move from comics to movies; of Marvel Studios; of non-white, non-male heroes; of Black Panther—and a smattering of superhero theory. I'll start there.

Among the myriad ways of defining genres, one could consider the kinds of bodies that populate them. The integral body of the cowboy is a fundament of the western; science fiction bodies might be astronauts, cyborgs, or aliens; musical bodies sing and dance; shadowy noir antiheroes cut through the shadowed spaces of the city; embodied monsters and their equally embodied victims haunt the worlds of horror; animated bodies squash and stretch.

If genres can be defined through the body, then superheroes are a genre on gamma rays, producing a seemingly unending set of variations on, and modifications of, the human body that embody a host of ambivalent and shifting attitudes toward flesh, self, technology, and society.

The superhero body incarnates ideas of race and ethnicity, queerness and hybridity, gender stereotypes and gender fluidity; it engages politics, vigilantism and masculinity, nationalism, social and individual responsibility, the divine and the monstrous. Superheroes embody technologies and attitudes toward technologies that encompass the industrial, atomic, electronic, biogenetic, and digital. There are still other, unsung, pleasures in the fantasy, pleasures that center upon superheroes as colorful, performative figures whose flamboyant self-presentation far exceeds the requirements of fighting crime.[1]

The superhero is explicitly and insistently embodied—the costumed super-body, on its own, defines the genre.

The superhero body also pushes beyond normative definitions; Scott Jeffery sees it as indisputably posthuman, generative and provisional: "a becoming, not a being."[2] He breaks the genre's corporealities into categories—the Perfect Body, the Cosmic Body, the Military-Industrial Body, Animal Bodies, and Artificial Bodies—while also leaving room for other configurations, such as Grotesque and Abject Bodies. Posthuman though they may be, superheroes coexist comfortably with non-super beings: only the villains advocate domination or radical separatism. Jeffery views the history of the genre as one of ongoing internal critique: more than simple "fascist parables" of American *Übermenschen* and might, these bodies are not singular in their meanings, and they can challenge ossifying fantasies of the invulnerable and the immutable.[3]

Superhero bodies are utopian constructions.

Richard Dyer's "Entertainment and Utopia," a deeply canonical text in the study of musicals, is pretty darn applicable to superheroes as well. Dyer located within the musical an energetic utopianism arising through representational and nonrepresentational elements: "Two of the taken-forgranted descriptions of entertainment, as 'escape' and as 'wish-fulfilment,' point to its central thrust, namely, utopianism. Entertainment offers the image of 'something better' to escape into, or something we want deeply that our day-to-day lives don't provide."[4] In terms that could as easily be applied to the corporeal imagination of superheroes, he writes, "Alternatives, hopes, wishes—these are the stuff of utopia, the sense that things could be better, that something other than what is can be imagined and maybe realised." Rather than map out "models of utopian worlds," entertainment presents "what utopia would *feel like*." In so doing, it "responds to real needs created by society," and its responses can be deeply self-contradictory, with, for example, narrative providing one kind of response or reconciliation and spectacular elements another.[5]

The musical's utopian affect shifts with time and treatment, but Dyer stresses the sense of *community* that can emerge, whether from narratives or just the synchronicity and harmony of audiovisual performance. *Brigadoon* (1947) is a good example, oddly relevant to *Black Panther*; it's a musical play about a mythic Scottish village that exists beyond the flow of history, featuring a tightly integrated score by Alan Jay Lerner and Frederick Loewe and choreography by Agnes de Mille, along with utopian community, performative harmony, and the "space apart" of the Broadway stage (an artifice preserved by the sound stages of the 1954 Hollywood adaptation directed by Vincente Minnelli). The plot involves American visitors, one enchanted, the other cynical, and a disaffected character who threatens the utopia's very existence.

Community isn't absent from the superhero genre—the super teams of the Avengers or Justice League, the extended Superman "family," and the substitute family of the X-Men all speak to communitarian desire—but the superhero's utopian affect is more fully expressed through each hero's unique embodiments: "the shapes of individual energies," as Leo Braudy

phrased it with regard to, again, musical performers.[6] Ramzi
Fawaz locates, in such groups as the New Mutants, the desire
for a community that won't constrain one's singularity.[7]

Superheroes are the site of an especially rich corporeal
imagination of "alternatives, hopes, [and] wishes." The body
of the superhero articulates everything from a child's desire
to defy gravity, to social anxieties around new technologies, to
traumatic social responses to oppressive structures of power
and control around race and gender. The superheroic imagination continually proffers "the image of 'something better' to
escape into . . . that our day-to-day lives don't provide."[8]

As one of the most exaggerated body narratives, superheroes
are particularly suited to phenomenological investigation. They
exemplify a corporeal imagination in which bodies encounter
the world in ways unavailable (I think) to the rest of us.

Phenomenology's ground is the perceiving, thinking, and
acting body that is the conduit for knowledge of the world beyond itself. As Maurice Merleau-Ponty writes, "Rather than a
mind and a body, man is a mind *with* a body, a being who can
only get to the truth of things because its body is, as it were,
embedded in those things."[9] To make sense of the world, we
regard it with *intent*, make judgments based on perceptual
*experience*, and test those perceptions and modify our expectations by moving our bodies into and through that world.
*Perception* and *motility* are the means of expressing and
directing purpose and effecting change. Subject and world
become self-modulating within a frame of meaningful action.

Superheroes embody fantasies of enhanced abilities in these
very areas—*perception*, *motility*, *action*. Black Panther's powers derive from the vibranium-infused, heart-shaped herb,

which, as N'Jobu (Sterling K. Brown) tells us in the prologue, gives him all the above: "superhuman strength, speed, and instincts." While scholars and skeptics have long obsessed over the genre's masculinist fantasies of vigilante justice or violence, superheroes, in presenting uniquely powerful ways of inhabiting space, world, and bodies, can encompass things far more resonant, something that can be further heightened in their expression through different media.

Every medium has its own ways of soliciting perceptual and corporeal engagement. But some pack a more powerful phenomenological wallop than others, and cinema must rank somewhere near the top. Cinema speaks to and reconstructs perceptual experience: it records photographically, magnifies through projection, refigures through editing, and embodies through movement—this last is urgent.

Like a human body and sensorium, a moving camera is limited to a single perspective that must perceive, engage, and explore the world in order to know it. The omniscience of narrative editing directs attention to pertinent details, but moving cameras and long takes more fully replicate the state of always partial knowledge in which "mortal men" find themselves. Camera movement can also partake of vehicular movement in ways familiar (a camera on a car) and transcendent (a camera in the nose of a rocket). Here, cinema offers a kind of super-embodiment that catapults viewers beyond quotidian perception without leaving "the body."

By definition, superheroes offer their own "super-embodiment." They embody, too, what we usually think of as technologies, with Superman's X-ray vision only the most obvious example. They are, then, at the same time human(ish) body, embodied technology, vehicle of movement, and enhanced perceptual apparatus. These super-bodies do a lot of conceptual super-lifting.

Comics accentuate the power of the superheroic body pictorially—though the scripts rarely expound upon the feeling of flying or phasing, the images revel in unfettered flight, dynamic movement, and physical triumph. Comics readers are shown, more than told, what it is to be a superhero. The level of abstraction imposed by drawing keeps the hero at a remove from the viewer; world and body are reduced to a static set of lines and unnaturally bright colors. The photo-realistic body grounds the cinematic superhero fantasy in the viewer's "reality" more fully than comics ever could (or should).

*Black Panther attacks.* Fantastic Four, *vol. 1, no. 52 (July 1966). Jack Kirby (pencils) and Joe Sinnott (inks).*

Black Panther dropping down to take out both the Thing *and* Mr. Fantastic with but a single Jack Kirby kick is thrilling; a movie car chase in which he, in slow motion, takes out an SUV and performs an elaborate series of flips that land him in a gentle feline crouch atop the car being virtually controlled by his sister, Shuri, is *thrilling*. I love the audaciousness of both, but cinema's ability to convey human movement and presence is unparalleled. Kirby's depiction of T'Challa reclining on his throne offers many things, but it doesn't offer the voice and body of Chadwick Boseman. Comic books reduce the size of the action; cinema, at least in its large formats, magnifies bodies and kinetic effect.

I write as a longtime skeptic: What could film possibly add to the already visual medium of comics? But I now see that superhero cinema, when it's working, can generate a more immediate relation to the heightened power(s) of the superhero body. Comics continue to offer myriad pleasures that movies don't—greater stylistic range, more diversified and extensive visual imaginations, ongoing reinterpretations and explorations, and the more intimate phenomenology of reading.[10] Still, movies offer that deeply compelling corporeal identification. The pleasures of superhero movies are numerous and audiences have responded: superheroes are central to popular culture in a way not seen since World War II—if then. The comics critic Tegan O'Neil summed up a new attitude when she wrote, "I arrived in the twenty-first century convinced that superheroes were dead and holding comics back"; the unprecedented popularity of the movies made her realize that "it wasn't that superheroes were holding comics back, but that comics were holding superheroes back."[11]

Teleological though it may sound, comic books were basically waiting for superheroes to happen.[12] Early comics, often used as promotional giveaways, reprinted comic strips; when the supply of those ran thin, publishers produced or contracted for original properties (usually copying those same strips). The first comic book with all new material was the oversize *New Fun*, published in 1935 by National Allied Publications, which would later become DC.

And then, in 1938, *behold the Superman*.

Superheroes gave the crudely printed four-color comic book something unique, and proved incredibly popular incredibly quickly. The superhero floodgates burst following the appearance of "The Batman" in May 1939, with the main superheroic archetypes established by 1941—the Golden Age of superheroes had commenced. World War II further fueled their popularity, and comics cannily exploited the patriotic mood: Superman, Captain America, and other star-spangled heroes went toe to toe with Axis spies. Soldiers, in need of cheap, portable entertainment, read comic books by the truckload.

The popularity of superheroes waned after the war; a broader range of genres was on offer to what were now becoming older comics readers. But they never really went away. Superman, Batman, and Wonder Woman continued to be featured in publications through the 1950s, and there were other signs of life as well (Timely Comics—later Marvel—tried to keep Captain America and Sub-Mariner afloat in the 1950s, now fighting Commies instead of Nazis, without much luck).

For a very long time, I resisted the superhero as a transmedial figure, seeing in them a pure expression of the possibilities of comics, the medium that birthed them. In the dim, dark past of 2001, on the cusp of the first X-Men and Spider-Man movies, the historian Bradford Wright wrote about what seemed to be the medium-specific nature of superheroes:

> Costumed superheroes had always been the stuff of comic books, and it really was the genre best suited to the

medium. In an era of extremely limited special-effects technology, comic books could present fantastic visual imagery more imaginatively than could a live-action medium. Individuals in tight, colorful costumes and masks performing impossible deeds simply looked ridiculous in live-action, but they seemed perfectly natural in comic books.[13]

And yet transmedial they were from early days, with Superman blazing the trail again and again. *Superman* comic books appeared in 1938; the following year saw the inception of the newspaper strip. He crossed into radio in 1940, animated shorts in 1941, and movie serials in 1948. The first superhero feature film, in 1951, was *Superman and the Mole Men* (Lee Sholem, 1951), which led to *Adventures of Superman* on TV in 1952. The year 1966 saw a slew of TV cartoons, not only DC and Marvel adaptations but some original offerings like *Space Ghost*. Superman got a Broadway musical in 1966 and a video game in 1979 (capitalizing on the success of Richard Donner's *Superman* in 1978). Nearly all of these were aimed at younger listeners and viewers. Radio and comic strips reached broader audiences, but superheroes in moving image media were, as they say, kiddie fare.

Wright was correct, though: special effects needed to achieve a certain perceptual plausibility for an adult audience to accept the on-screen superhero. The tagline for *Superman* was "You'll believe a man can fly," but the effects weren't nearly convincing enough for that (even at the time) so, y'know, we really didn't. But, and this is important, Christopher Reeve somehow did *not* look ridiculous in the costume, and he was so compelling and charming and relaxed a presence that what you believed was that perhaps there could really be a Superman.[14] With the development of ever more sophisticated CGI technologies that could seamlessly integrate effects with recorded images, and live actors with animation, the twenty-first-century superhero movie emerged. Just as the flat, four-color medium of comics was perfect for the presentation of these primary-colored do-gooders, so did digital effects prove ideal in presenting hybridized bodies that were both human and more than human.[15] The standard joke was that special effects had to catch up with what Jack Kirby had been doing on paper fifty years earlier.

Now that they have become visually plausible enough to pass muster, the phenomenologically powerful, hugely technologized medium of the cinema has become something of the superhero's natural home; but it's worth restating that *both* of the most successful incarnations of superheroes were functions of their respective technologies: four-color printing for comics and digital effects for cinema.

At the tail end of the 1950s, DC brought back revamped versions of older heroes like the Flash and Green Lantern as well as a host of new ones. Marvel followed suit, and other companies, including Archie and Charlton, introduced superheroes of their own. DC's comics were visually attractive and sometimes narratively compelling (Mort Weisinger's Superman Family comics were among the best) but left untouched the classic superhero formula: noble heroes doing noble things. They were a bit square, more or less the same character in differently colored tights.

But then, in 1961, *behold the Fantastic Four*.

Marvel took the genre in new directions. Stan Lee was the

editor and main writer for the company through the 1950s, cranking out genre yarns by the yard. Spurred by the success of DC's *Justice League of America*, he and publisher Martin Goodman decided to try their own superhero team. *Fantastic Four* was a collaboration between Lee and artist Jack Kirby (co-creator, with Joe Simon, of Captain America in 1940), and it was immediately different from DC's offerings—the characters had distinct personalities and didn't always get along. The comic also gave us the Thing—the first superhero who didn't welcome the deforming changes to his body, a seismic shift in the genre.

Expanding the superheroic concept to encompass gods, monsters, and kings, Marvel rolled out an astonishing roster of memorable characters in short order: the Hulk, the return of Sub-Mariner, Spider-Man, Thor, Ant-Man (all in 1962); Iron Man, Doctor Strange, the Avengers, the X-Men, Nick Fury—as both WWII-era Howling Commando *and* contemporary S.H.I.E.L.D. super-spy (1963); Daredevil, the return of Captain America (1964); the Inhumans (1965); Black Panther, Silver Surfer, and Galactus (1966). These heroes and antiheroes were both weirder and more human than their forebears, and Lee's dialogue ranged in tone from Ben Grimm's Brooklynese to the florid, faux-Shakespearian elocutions of Asgardians and galactic heralds (culminating in Iron Man's snarky question upon meeting Thor in *Avengers* [Joss Whedon, 2012]: "Doth Mother know you weareth her drapes?").

Before Marvel, superhero stories were short, a few per issue, peppered with the occasional "novel-length" adventure. Marvel largely began with full-length stories and introduced two-parters that began in one issue and finished in the next.[16] This not only built suspense (and sold more comics); it made possible more complex stories that helped attract older readers. Stories might even begin in one superhero title and end in another.

Marvel's weren't the first heroes to share the occasional adventure, but, uniquely, they shared a reality: pretty much all the heroes lived in New York, and events in one book had repercussions for another (back then, when things happened in the Marvel Universe—marriages, deaths—they *stayed* happened). Even if readers didn't buy every comic, they knew that life went on beyond the pages of any single one, whereas DC stories occurred in that temporal zone Umberto Eco called "an ever-continuing present."[17] Where superheroes had inhabited closed and limited worlds, Marvel opened things up: the emergent network of references accumulated into something that became known as "continuity."[18]

At the highest level, continuity in superhero universes includes more than the totality of all existing stories; Richard Reynolds proposes that it further "embraces those actions which are not recorded in any specific text, but inescapably implied."[19] Just because we've never *seen* Superman's grandfather, to use Reynolds's example, it doesn't mean he didn't have one, and, moreover, one who might appear at any moment in the comics, in the movies, or, just as crucially, in the minds of Superman fans. There is, as Reynolds notes, something mythic about this never-ending, ever-expanding saga, constantly forming and re-forming in the minds of devout readers and viewers. Along the way, it produced a history, nay, a *Universe*.

Audience investment is fundamental to this sense of universe, and it emerges in part from the serial nature of superhero fiction—first in comics, then in cinema—where, as Frank Kelleter writes, reception "does not distinctly 'follow' the production and publication of a finished text," but rather offers "a particularly close entanglement of production and reception."[20] Fans respond to the latest installment of an ongoing superhero saga via letters to the editor, YouTube videos, or message boards; companies respond, feeding information, changing directions, and hiding Easter eggs that would escape the notice of all but the most committed fans. All of this generates some pretty intense "affective bonds" among readers and viewers of superhero (and other serial) fictions who have come to feel that they have a stake in the development of this proliferating universe.[21] In recent years, this has been tainted by misogynist or white supremacist subgroups (discussed below), but it was foundational to the success of Marvel Comics and the Marvel Cinematic Universe. DC soon followed, and universes *themselves* proliferated.

Moving beyond its original Cold War Manichaean worldview, Marvel got hip. College students wrote letters of fulsome praise; some were featured in *Esquire* magazine in 1966. Lee became something of a counterculture media celebrity, blithely aligning his comics with such movements as Pop Art. He expanded on techniques pioneered by other comics publishers: contributors were credited and there were humorous features about them. Everything was presented in a jokey, just-between-us tone. There was a fan club, letters pages, and, most audaciously, Stan's Soapbox, where—not unlike Hugh Hefner in *Playboy*—Lee opined on the issues of the day, but mostly on all things Marvel. The company was reaching new audiences while making them feel part of something special. (It sure worked for me.) The Marvel Universe was more than a function of interrelated characters and narratives; it encompassed the relation of readers to Marvel Comics itself.

By the mid-'60s, Marvel was selling itself as antiestablishment without being overly political. Heroes were constantly

chiding activists to be less disruptive (Thor's advice to a buncha
hippies, for example, is that " 'Tis not by **dropping out**—but
by **plunging in**—into the maelstrom of **life** itself—that thou
shalt find thy **wisdom!**"), and activist groups were constantly
being infiltrated by insidious forces (when in real life they were
being infiltrated by the FBI).[22] There were more Black supporting characters and bystanders (one letter writer unironically
praised Marvel for acknowledging the existence of the "Negro
race").[23] Also on the rise was the use of the "mutant" X-Men as
proxies in allegorical stories about bigotry and discrimination.

And then, in 1966, *behold the Black Panther.*

Fantastic Four, *vol. 1, no. 52 (July 1966). Jack
Kirby (pencils), Joe Sinnott (inks).*

The character first appeared in a two-part story in *Fantastic Four*.[24] A mysterious "African chieftain" sends a mysteriously high-tech aircraft to bring the super-team to his nation of Wakanda. "But," wonders the Thing in an oft-quoted line, "how does some refugee from a Tarzan movie lay his hands on **this** kinda gizmo?" In Wakanda the team is dazzled by an electronic jungle, strikingly depicted by Jack Kirby (more about this in the Wakanda chapter), but is nonplussed when the chieftain, in the guise of Black Panther, attacks. Turns out it was just a test of his abilities, and by the end of part 1, leader Reed Richards is convinced of the Panther's honorable motives.

Next issue, T'Challa and his guests, all friends now, gather as he tells them of the "tragic curse" he lives under: when he was a boy, Ulysses Klaw (which is how they spelled it in the comics) killed his father, King T'Chaka, who stood between Klaw and the vibranium mound he wanted to plunder. T'Challa, in short order, swore vengeance, turned Klaw's own super-weapon upon the invading force, and took up the mantle of Black Panther. He later used vibranium to amass a fortune, send himself to "the fine universities of both hemispheres," and build what the Thing called "that far-out mechanized jungle of yours." The Thing, a guy who's seen "a million jungle movies," is bored by T'Challa's description of idyllic pre-Klaw Wakanda: "I know the rest by **heart**! Everything wuz hunky dory until the greedy **ivory hunters** made the scene!" Before we get too excited by Lee and Kirby's anti-colonialist fervor, coming on the very heels of Rhodesian independence, we should remember that this was indeed the plot of the 1934 movie *Tarzan and His Mate*.[25]

Lee and Kirby played up the anachronistic relation of high-tech and African jungle. In this early iteration, T'Challa likes his pleasures—commanding servants, lighting up cigarettes, and residing in luxury ("Wow! Wotta pad!" the Thing enthuses. "I'll bet even Hugh Hefner couldn't improve on **this** layout!"). With the defeat of Klaw and his solid sound menagerie (don't ask), the Fantastic Four convinces the Panther to use his powers for the good of the world, paving the way for his entry into the Marvel Universe.[26]

Readers, already hip to Marvel's hipness, responded with enthusiasm. One celebrated the appearance of "a real life Negro superhero!!!"[27]

Black Panther became a more established figure when he joined the Avengers (beginning in *Avengers* #52, May 1968),

*Diminutive T'Challa.* The Avengers, *vol. 1, no. 58 (November 1968). John Buscema (art).*

the stories scripted by Roy Thomas. He came and went from the group, and when he appeared on the covers he was often diminutive, in the background with other second-stringers. But there were sporadic attempts to do something more with the character, usually around issues of race. He even took on a secret identity as a Harlem school teacher to better understand the challenges of the inner city.

Black Panther was followed, in 1966, by the Falcon; a Black Green Lantern and Luke Cage both appeared in 1972, and Black Lightning showed up in 1978. Ramzi Fawaz situates this group of heroes as part of a decade-long period he's dubbed "the urban folktale," which sought "to reassert the superhero as a uniquely American icon" against the dual contexts of a "conceptually bankrupt" national character and the celebration of racial and ethnic diversity.[28] Moving Black Panther on up to Harlem tied him to this streetwise bunch.

These heroes were all about Black pride.[29] The Panther was a king and John Stewart (the Black Green Lantern) less subservient to his intergalactic police "mission." The Falcon was a partner-slash-sidekick to Captain America; Steve Engelhart's scripts had them negotiate and navigate their roles and the significance of their racial dynamic (Black Panther later gave him, literally and metaphorically, wings).[30] Luke Cage, acutely aware of his lower-class status, wasn't too proud to be a "hero for hire."[31]

When the civil rights era demanded more superheroic diversity, it fell to the existing stable of white writers and artists to provide the material. *Luke Cage: Hero for Hire,* the first series to star a Black hero, was created by Roy Thomas, Archie Goodwin, and John Romita, all white men, in the mold of such blaxploitation heroes as *Shaft* (Gordon Parks, 1971) and *Superfly* (Gordon Parks Jr., 1972). Neither Marvel nor DC had a deep enough bench to supply top-tier Black writers and artists, but they did understand the need, and there followed a slow influx of Black creators. African American artist Billy Graham inked the first issue of *Luke Cage* and moved between penciling and inking the book's sixteen-issue run; he also co-plotted. Another Black artist on *Luke Cage* (with Cage's new moniker of Power Man), Trevor von Eeden, co-created and illustrated *Black Lightning*, the first DC series to star a Black hero.[32] More Black comics creators emerged in the 1980s, and in 1991 Dwayne McDuffie, Denys Cowan, Michael Davis, and Derek T. Dingle formed Milestone Comics, a DC affiliate that featured a slate of superheroes of color, including Icon, Static, Hardware, and the super-team Blood Syndicate.[33]

Black Panther's first solo story arc was a signal moment for the character and, too, for superhero fiction. "Panther's Rage" was scripted with typical verbosity by Don McGregor, a one-time proofreader who oversaw *Jungle Action*, a reprint-only book that he described as "basically blond jungle gods and goddesses saving the native populace from whatever threat. It was pretty racist stuff."[34] He pitched a story and, as with many a failing comics title, editorial was willing to experiment. In "Panther's Rage," McGregor crafted the longest saga in Marvel (and superhero) history to that point. He refused to use either white guest heroes (a reliable method of goosing sales) or a white supporting cast. The book was originally penciled by Rich Buckler, an unabashed Kirby clone, but with the fourth chapter Billy Graham took over, becoming more visually audacious with each issue.

*Killmonger and Panther at Warrior Falls.* Jungle
Action, *vol. 2, no. 17 (September 1975). Billy
Graham (art).*

McGregor centered the action in Wakanda, mapping it,
populating it, and giving it, for the first time, a history. He did
the same for the Panther, deepening his motivations and exploring the whole "king of Wakanda" aspect that had been kept
in the background (so he could run off and join the Avengers).

In "Panther's Rage," T'Challa returns to his homeland to face rebellious countrymen who regard him as a sellout and have turned to a demagogue, Erik Killmonger, who has fed and exploited their growing doubt. In the letters pages, the new subtleties of Wakanda get lots of attention. A reader praises the work as "revolutionary" in that "Africans in Africa" were shown to be "different from Afro-Americans."[35] Another letter writer speaks for Wakanda's unique historical and cultural status: "It is encouraging to know it has withstood the on-slaught of white hunters, jungle girls, and Tarzan-types, and has remained a settlement of BLACK people in the African jungle."[36] Ralph Macchio, a future writer and editor at Marvel, concurred, praising the depictions "of the inner workings of an all-Black society."[37]

The story throws the character back upon himself, forc-ing him to explore his competing loyalties: Is he responsible to the primarily white, American-centric Avengers? Or to Wakanda, whose cultural unity is badly eroding? In this, the story resonates with the urban folktale model that Fawaz situ-ates in the 1970–1975 period ("Panther's Rage" began in 1973): the story isn't urban, it's not about redefining citizenship, but it participates in a similar revisionism by rethinking the precepts of the character.

The subsequent comics creators who made the most con-sequential contributions to the mythos of the Black Panther were African American. Christopher Priest gave the world a streetwise, blaxploitation-inflected Panther with glam female bodyguards—the Dora Milaje—who were also, ickily, the king's "wives-in-waiting." Priest also introduced a bumbling white character, American liaison Everett Ross, who narrated the stories hyperbolically, hilariously, and nonlinearly.

*An urbane Panther with the Dora Milaje (wives-in-waiting).* Black Panther, *vol. 3, no. 1 (November 1998). Mark Texeira (art).*

Ross was meant as a conduit for white audiences; it was a canny move, but one that underscored something about T'Challa: he's often presented as aloof, isolated. It's hard to be the king, and many are the times when the crown sits heavily upon T'Challa's head—but it also seems to weigh upon the writers of *Black Panther* comics. Back in 1955, the director Howard Hawks explained the failure of his historical epic *Land of the Pharaohs* by admitting, "I don't know how a Pharaoh talks," and it's a good bet that most comics writers don't know how African kings might talk or behave (Stan Lee gave T'Challa one of his "literary" voices: " *'Twas I who invited you for the hunt!*").[38] Thor may have been a god, but he was committed to his beloved "Midgard" (Earth), and his boisterous personal qualities were eminently relatable ("I make grave mistakes all the time," he all-too-cheerfully confesses in *Thor: Ragnarok*).

Small wonder that Black Panther has, variously, joined the Avengers, taken on a secret identity as an inner-city schoolteacher, married Storm of the X-Men, led the Fantastic Four, and taken over Daredevil's protector role in Hell's Kitchen. Small wonder he's often been surrounded by more "relatable" characters, be they white, African, or African American. Ta-Nehisi Coates turned Wakanda into a representative democracy with a largely ceremonial monarchy. He has said that "T'Challa doesn't actually like being a king," but it's the Panther's writers that seem to have had the biggest problem with it.[39]

Coates admitted in a podcast that the difficulty of writing T'Challa was that he was created as a kind of "paper-cutout propaganda piece against racism," too perfect in every way, without the kind of flaws that made Marvel heroes so compelling.[40] Wesley Morris, co-host of said podcast, compares him to the kind of characters Sidney Poitier played in the 1960s: each was "a white invention" that incarnated "the most perfect"—and least offensive to whites—"specimen of Blackness."[41]

McGregor took the "king" part seriously, but his Panther wasn't much of a *superhero*—he was constantly beaten, battered, and bleeding.[42] The Wakanda of "Panther's Rage" was more a political than a technological entity. Priest brought back the tech but kept the Panther in the States for long stretches (this was when we found out that Panther had joined the Avengers to spy on them, a plot twist sassily reversed by Coates, whose Panther admits, "I spied for my country in order to join the Avengers").[43]

Priest tried to boost sales by including that white mediator and recruiting superhero guest stars aplenty. The Panther's next major writer, filmmaker Reginald Hudlin (who would later direct Chadwick Boseman in *Marshall* [2017]), conversely noted that the pervasive crossover, in the 1990s, of Black cultural forms and figures into white culture showed that "the masses of young people of all races who grew up with hip hop's symbolic posturing of unapologetic Black male prowess" were ready, if not hungry, for a more Afro-centric version of Black Panther and Wakanda.[44]

Gone was the white guy mediator. The Dora Milaje no longer catered to the male gaze; Hudlin and John Romita Jr. offered a new look that stressed their warrior status, turning them into the "Grace Jones–lookin' chicks" (as they're referred to) of the movie. And Wakanda's pride and unconquerable power were shown to greatly predate the fortuitous appearance of vibranium.[45] Hudlin's Wakanda was more engaged with world politics, providing surreptitious support for anti-apartheid groups and Tutsi rebels. The debate around the country's isolationist policy, which drives the movie, was foregrounded during Marvel's *Civil War* crossover comics event, which explored the relation between superheroes and the state.

Coates took the *Black Panther* comic in a few new directions: the Wakandan government was restructured, T'Challa found himself in a blast of an Afrofuturist transgalactic space opera, and a blaxploitation homage teamed him with Luke Cage, Misty Knight, and the rest of "The Crew." Coates also worked with other notable Black writers, including Roxane Gay, to expand upon Wakanda's history, its culture, and especially its women; in the wake of the *Black Panther* movie, the Afrofuturist science fiction writer Nnedi Okorafor scripted new adventures for Shuri.[46]

*Space opera.* Black Panther, *vol. 7, no. 1 (May 2018).*
*Daniel Acuña (art).*

The screenplay for *Black Panther*, co-written by Coogler and
Joe Robert Cole, incorporated narrative, visual, and conceptual
elements from all of these iterations: high-tech Wakanda from
Lee and Kirby, Killmonger and Warrior Falls from McGregor,

the Dora Milaje and Everett Ross from Priest, a richer Wakandan history and politics from Hudlin, and strong female characters and an upgraded Panther costume from Coates (with artist Brian Stelfreeze).

Meanwhile, in the transmedial world of superheroes, Tim Burton's *Batman* (1989) and *Batman Returns* (1992) confirmed the existence of an older audience for superhero movies, and the 1990s were marked by sporadic attempts to build on that success. DC's preexisting synergy with Warner Media (as it's now known), its corporate owner since 1990, helped it forge an efficient transmedial presence. Marvel, under rapacious management, stumbled badly in the '90s, entering bankruptcy in 1996. Licensing its characters to outside movie studios infused the company with cash. Marvel made money off bombs and blockbusters alike, but the hits made *way more* money for the other studios than they ever would for Marvel. In the absence of creative oversight, control, or an aggressive media strategy, the company was in danger of squandering its legacy. Forming its own production unit addressed the problems, and in 2005 Marvel Studios announced the self-financing of a slate of films based on characters not already licensed out, including Black Panther. Kevin Feige became president of production as the company began work on *Iron Man* (with director Jon Favreau).[47]

The success of this venture was hardly a foregone conclusion. Marvel had licensed away some of its best known characters (Spider-Man!), and DC had staked out the "adult" market by playing up the grimmer side of the superhero life and giving creative latitude to such directors as Burton and Christopher Nolan.

Marvel's approach would be different. The company played up the continuity between its historical innovations in comics and what it could do on screen.[48] There was the shared universe, which led to the insanely ambitious plan for an interconnected set of blockbusters that would tease their way to a culmination in *The Avengers*. The movies showed a bit of cheek, a brightness and playfulness that recalled the irreverent freshness of the original comics. The filmmakers and actors came across as fans intent on "getting it right," but there was a concurrent winnowing of sixty years of unwieldy continuity to make the movies more accessible. They also wooed a bunch of not-entirely-mainstream auteurs, like Taika Waititi, Chloé Zhao, and Ryan Coogler. And there was the public face of Marvel Studios, Kevin Feige, inheriting the mantle of devotee-ringleader that Stan Lee had worn.[49]

Through these strategies Marvel Studios established itself as the most responsible caretaker for those characters, these stories, and this universe. The authors of *The Marvel Studios Phenomenon* wrote, "As the page-turning imagery in Marvel's iconic logo announces with each film text, a notion of stories, rooted in print origins, remains the symbol of the company's artistic compact with audiences. The logo signifies both a source point for stories/characters, and a hallmark of quality control."[50] The studio created a narrative about itself that satisfied devoted fans and a skeptical industry, and Marvel itself was that story.

*The ever-changing Marvel Studios logo.*

*       *       *

Twenty-first-century superhero movies from DC and Marvel were slow to diversify their characters beyond sidekicks, supporting players, love interests, and those permitted to briefly wear the costume—not until *Black Panther* did a superhero of color from a major franchise headline a movie. Of course the glue holding the MCU together was Samuel L. Jackson's Nick Fury, so there's that.[51] Diversifying supporting casts was laudatory but low risk; putting non-white, non-male heroes front and center in $200 million-plus productions was more of a gamble. That studios, eyeing the bottom line, weren't racing to rectify the problem didn't come as a shock.

In the end, they needn't have worried. Around ten years into the superhero cycle, there arrived a spate of successful films starring and directed and/or written by People Who Aren't All White and Male: *Wonder Woman* (Patty Jenkins, 2017), *Black Panther* (2018), the underrated *Captain Marvel* (Anna Boden and Ryan Fleck, 2019), and *Birds of Prey (and the Fantabulous Emancipation of One Harley Quinn)* (written by Christina Hodson and directed with panache by Cathy Yan, 2020). The growing number of television superheroes added further breadth, bringing Supergirl, Jessica Jones, Luke Cage, the lesbian version of Batwoman, an animated version of Harley Quinn, and some diversely peopled super-teams.

The desire to bring Black Panther to the screen predated the incorporation of Marvel Studios.[52] In the 1990s, Wesley Snipes, in the first flush of his popularity, proposed a Panther movie, envisioning it as a corrective to Hollywood's general mistreatment of Africa—Wakanda, then, was always part of the story. Snipes planned the movie to follow *Demolition Man* (Marco Brambilla, 1993), which I mention only because I really love *Demolition Man*. Snipes was negotiating with

Stan Lee and with Columbia Studios, and was in discussions with such writer/directors as Mario Van Peebles and John Singleton. Snipes gained further credibility after his *Blade* movies (horror-superhero fusions) practically saved Marvel financially, but apparently they never came up with a script that satisfied Lee.

Finally, Marvel Studios announced *Black Panther* in 2014, with plans for a release three years later. Boseman had already been cast as the Panther in *Captain America: Civil War* (without an audition—it does seem a no-brainer), and Marvel, in particular Nate Moore, its lone African American producer, set out to put together a more diverse production crew than it usually fielded. Ava DuVernay was mentioned, but the creative visions never matched.[53] Coogler seemed a good bet in the wake of his commercial success with *Creed* (2015) and signed on with the stipulation that he could keep the movie more personal by bringing actors and crew, many of color, from his previous productions. The movie that resulted was a huge hit with the Marvel crowd but reached well beyond the usual demographic, garnering a fervent African American audience that cut across gender and age, and here we are.

Before *Black Panther* landed on the scene, common wisdom had it that blockbuster movies with Black leads or Black creators wouldn't perform as strongly, domestically or internationally, as more "traditional" entries. And while there's some debate about how to define Black movies or art—is it a matter of personnel or subject matter?—Hollywood seemed to have a clear idea: a Black movie was a movie that pretty much only Black people saw. It was a not insignificant demographic to be sure, but a drop in the global moviegoing bucket.

That was, on the face of it, nonsense—Denzel, at least, could open a movie, and mass audiences seemed fine with Snipes as Blade, to take but two examples. But that was the common wisdom, and it restricted who got to star and write and direct. But change happens. In 2019, Lawrence Ware of the *New York Times* proclaimed the past decade to have been, as the title of his article indicates, "the most important decade for movies about Black lives," citing examples like *Creed* (Ryan Coogler, 2016), *Moonlight* (Barry Jenkins, 2016), and *Selma* (Ava DuVernay, 2014).[54]

*Black Panther*, then, didn't come out of nowhere. It helped that too-white Hollywood was becoming aware of its problem, and was starting to open the doors (a crack) to a wider range of practitioners. It helped that established Black talent, like Forest Whitaker, founded production companies that championed young filmmakers who drew upon more diversified casts and crew to make movies about Black life, like Coogler did with *Fruitvale Station* (2013). It helped that Blacker movies were begetting more movies, and that more diverse audiences were responding to them. It helped that there were writers and directors willing to go mainstream without sacrificing their concern with Black lives.

Yet there still had been no blockbuster movie helmed by a non-male, non-white director, so "common wisdom" still held. But where could such a blockbuster property come from? Who would take that multi-hundred-million-dollar risk?

Well, it helped that Marvel Studios, a new studio with some fresh ideas, had, by releasing a couple of blockbusters every year, created a juggernaut called the Marvel Cinematic Universe that badly needed to move away from the white, male heroes at its center. And it helped that Marvel owned

an awesome character that was the very first Black superhero
from a major comics publisher.

Marvel recognized *Black Panther*'s potential to reach new
audiences, and it marketed the film accordingly. It primed
the pump in 2016 by introducing the character in *Captain
America: Civil War*, and featured Boseman and Coogler at
Comic-Con in San Diego. The teaser trailer premiered in
mid-2017 during game 4 of the NBA finals on ABC, then was
released to social media, where it generated a staggering 89
million views in twenty-four hours.[55] Kendrick Lamar (and
a host of collaborators) released *Black Panther: The Album*.
The world tour to promote the movie included stops in Africa. Coogler talked up the personal aspects of the project
while trailers promoted its spectacle. Disney Consumer
Products tapped a set of carefully curated designers to create
Wakanda-inspired fashions for an "immersive display" during
New York Fashion Week.[56]

Did it work? Yup.

The movie opened *big*, and it stayed big for a long time—a
matter of months, not weeks—shattering records as it went.
Within a month it had grossed a billion dollars.[57] Some of the
significant records broken by *Black Panther* include: most tick-
ets sold in advance; biggest February opening weekend; biggest
non-sequel opening weekend; biggest solo superhero launch of
all time; biggest opening weekend ever for any movie not directed by a white guy; second-biggest superhero movie opening
weekend; fifth-highest-grossing superhero movie; most diverse
North American audience ever for a superhero movie; first superhero movie nominated for Best Picture by the Motion Picture Academy for Arts and Sciences.[58] The movie, for Bryan
Rolli (writing for *Forbes*), "raise[d] a defiant, razor-clawed

middle finger to the ridiculous Hollywood notion that actors and directors of color are less bankable than their white male counterparts."[59]

So there was no blockbuster with Black leads and directors, until there was. And it was a doozy.[60] But what was more deeply remarkable was the way the movie was, as Carvell Wallace put it, "steeped very specifically and purposefully in its blackness."[61] James Wilt wrote:

> Black Panther didn't have to be a "political" film. Its trailer didn't have to feature Gil Scott-Heron's legendary poem "The Revolution Will Not Be Televised." The opening scene didn't have to take place in an apartment littered with Public Enemy posters, in Oakland (the home of the Black Power movement), in 1992—the very year of the Rodney King riots. The film's villain didn't have to be explicitly motivated by fierce desire for armed Pan-African insurrection against colonialism, white supremacy and mass incarceration. But it did.[62]

The cultural importance of *Black Panther* was evident from the start but also evolved over time. There were three waves of articles on the movie's importance. The first was anticipatory—focusing on the first superhero movie directed by a Black director, the first to star a Black superhero from a major franchise. Wallace wrote from his home of Oakland, days before *Panther* opened there, thinking back to Coogler's *Fruitvale Station* at the same theater. He conversed with Coogler about the distance between Africa and African Americans, and ended by writing, "We seek to make a place where we belong."[63]

The next wave of articles followed in the days, weeks, and

first months following the movie's release on February 16, 2018. *Forbes* seemed to have an article a day charting the path of *Black Panther* as it shattered one box office record after another. Sidebar pieces reflected on Wakanda's women—their humor, their leadership styles—what *Black Panther* offered transportation theorists, how it changed Hollywood (diversity sells!) and how it didn't (one movie ain't enough!), and so on.[64]

The third wave followed Boseman's death, which provided the opportunity to think about *Black Panther*'s impact two years after its release. Here, in the depths of the COVID-19 lockdown, dealing with a disease that disproportionately affected people who were Black, brown, and lower-income, the very image of Black positivity and possibility was gone. Adults and their children struggled with the news.[65] Through Boseman's absence, the importance of *Black Panther* came solidly into view. Playing American heroes, he had become one.

*Black Panther*, then, was evolutionary *and* revolutionary. Where do we go from here? Well, my future self has already seen what is, for my present self, the forthcoming *Black Panther 2: Wakanda Forever* (hope I liked it!). There's also the Wakanda television series being produced by Coogler and his Proximity Media company. *The Falcon and The Winter Soldier* worked for Disney+. More important, Coogler's generation of filmmakers is paying it forward, producing work for other up-and-comers (Coogler produced Shaka King's *Judas and the Black Messiah*, for example, and Ava DuVernay has been mentoring so many people that the *New York Times* published an article about it).[66]

Despite Black Panther's presence in other Marvel movies, *Black Panther* stands comfortably on its own. I confessed my own bias toward self-contained aesthetic works in the introduction, but come on, I'm hardly immune to the pleasures of serialized superhero stories. The rest of this book will explore the movie more or less on its own terms, so let's here consider *Black Panther* in the context of the Marvel Cinematic Universe.

When I rewatched many Marvel movies in prepping for this book, *Black Panther*'s genre trappings were thrown into sharp relief. At the end of *Iron Man* (Jon Favreau, 2008), Tony Stark acknowledges his secret identity, announcing, "I am Iron Man." T'Challa outs himself to the authorities in *Civil War* and seems about to do so to the world at the end of *Black Panther*. His moral gravitas and nationalist identification align him with Captain America—in the climactic battle in *Avengers: Endgame*, as Captain America stands alone and on the edge of defeat before Thanos, all the heroes who had "died" at Thanos's hand (or finger-snap) return; T'Challa leads the way.

Killmonger has echoes of the Winter Soldier—Bucky Barnes, Captain America's first sidekick—who had served for decades as a brainwashed, trained assassin.[67] Killmonger murders for the United States, Barnes for Hydra. Through most of *Civil War*, T'Challa holds Barnes responsible for killing his father; after he discovers his error, he offers Barnes safe haven in Wakanda. The first appearance of Wakanda in the MCU occurs in the post-credit sequence of *Civil War*; the final post-credit scene in *Black Panther* returns us to Barnes, still there.

*Civil War* also features the first appearance of CIA agent Everett Ross (Martin Freeman), and his "good guy" role in *Black Panther* proved so polarizing that it warrants attention. *Black Panther* was faulted for aligning Wakanda with the CIA, and for including a white character with whom white audiences would presumably "identify." It's true that Ross comes out of the Priest-scripted Panther comics, where that was his function. But that's not his role in the movie. All of his *oohs* and *aahs* about what Wakandan technology hath wrought mark him, in part, as the "white witness," Valerie Babb's term for characters in early Black speculative fiction who "place a white audience in alternative perspectival shoes so they might see the errors of their racist ways"—a more progressive function than just being the "likable white guy."[68] And he's not in Wakanda as a CIA agent but because he's taken a bullet for Nakia of the Wakandan team during an attempt to capture Ulysses Klaue (Andy Serkis)—now with a less comic-booky spelling of his name—and there is nary a hint that he would ever betray those who have saved his life at no small risk to themselves or to their nation. He joins with Ramonda (T'Challa's mother, played by Angela Bassett), Nakia (Lupita Nyong'o), and Shuri (Letitia Wright) to save Wakanda but shows no inclination to take charge. Ross is also the butt of the movie's best joke. M'Baku, of the Jabari Tribe, commands his silence in the most savage terms: "One more *word*," he thunders, "and I will *feed* you to my *children*." Ross visibly gulps. M'Baku lightens the mood: "I'm kidding. We are vegetarians." M'Baku (a wonderful Winston Duke) laughs himself silly. I have to say, it was worth bringing Ross to Wakanda just for that, and for the moment when Shuri derisively calls him "colonizer." Finally, Ross serves as the token white man, sidelined from the main action and always a step or two behind.[69] On the movie poster, Ross is diminutive, off in a corner—just as the token Black Panther was situated on many an *Avengers* cover.

*Black Panther* is perhaps most like *Thor* and its sequels.

Neither Thor nor Black Panther is a traditional superhero—
one's a god, the other's a king. Like Thor, Black Panther is
the heir to a throne. The mythic-futuristic Asgard is a separate realm of visual marvels: visually and conceptually a pre-
cursor to Wakanda. *Thor: Ragnarok*, directed by Indigenous
filmmaker Taika Waititi, engaged Asgard's repressed history
of bloody conquest, anticipating *Panther*'s anti-colonialism
and the erasure of N'Jobu's son from Wakandan history. The
endless maneuvers of Thor's trickster half-brother, Loki, to
take the throne anticipates T'Challa's cousin, Killmonger, who,
when asked what he wants, snaps simply, "I want the throne."
But beyond its considerable entertainment value, there are no
real-world stakes in the jousting of Thor and Loki for Odin's
favor. Asgard is not on Earth, and the problems of gods, like
the familial jousting on TV shows like *Dynasty* or *Succession*,
exist at a safe remove from such mere mortals as us.

*Black Panther* also connects to the Marvel Cinematic Universe
in that it is neither the first nor the last movie in which the
character—to this point played by Boseman—appears.

*Captain America: Civil War* stages the obligatory traumatic
superhero origin story but moves the trauma to T'Challa's
adulthood. King T'Chaka is assassinated in what seems a ter-
rorist bombing as he speaks to a United Nations convocation
concerning superheroes and the state. T'Challa is in atten-
dance, and we find him first conversing with Black Widow.
Boseman restrains his signature charm as befits his diplomatic
mission, and his accent is thicker than it will be in *Black Panther*. T'Chaka, before his speech, cradles his son's face in his
hand; it will be their last living contact. In the bombing's immediate aftermath, T'Challa crawls to his father's body and

cradles it in his arms. These images will recur when T'Challa
ascends to the Ancestral Plane in *Black Panther*.

From here, T'Challa is on a mission of vengeance (like his
comics forebear), and Boseman's performance is *cold*. In the
action scenes, the Panther talks little and attacks much, in the
martial arts fashion of the other earth-bound Avengers, like
Black Widow or Captain America. In the mega-superhero airport battle, he's more or less one more costumed character in a
physically low-stakes, verbally high-banter slugfest. He offers
not a single quip. Compare this to another superhero introduced in *Civil War*: Tom Holland's iteration of Spider-Man,
who steals the scene with his wide-eyed naivete. Spider-Man
is nothing but ingratiating; in contrast, Black Panther is once
more another second-string Avenger.

I originally found little of interest in *Civil War*, apart from
that remarkably entertaining airport free-for-all, but it gains
resonance in retrospect: to see, in "real time," the scenes of
T'Chaka's death and T'Challa's grief is so much more painful.
And the Panther's mission of single-minded revenge for the
assassination of his father anticipates Killmonger's own quest—
with a difference. The assassin's family had been collateral
damage from an Avengers action; knowing he cannot destroy
them, he seeks to get them to destroy themselves. "Vengeance
has consumed you," T'Challa tells him. "It's consuming them.
I'm done letting it consume me."[70] Killmonger will not make
that choice.

Nevertheless, Boseman's Panther made little impact on me
in this initial foray. The humorlessness of the character fore-
shadows not at all his style in *Black Panther*, and there is no
sense of Wakanda's cultural uniqueness. It takes *Black Panther*
all of a minute and a half into T'Challa's first scene to get to

some warm banter with the general of the Dora Milaje, Okoye (Danai Gurira), with a Boseman smile tossed in for good measure. My response was different to *Infinity War*, which was post-*Panther*. *Infinity War* takes us back to Wakanda, and our first view of Bast and the Golden City is accompanied by the familiar fanfare theme from Ludwig Göransson's *Panther* score. So it isn't just Black Panther that has a place in the story, as in *Civil War*; Okoye, Shuri, M'Baku, and their homeland are equally venerated. The movie fully assimilates what we might call the Panther Universe into the MCU.

It's really nice to see everyone again in this all-star superhero super-spectacular, but our understanding of the characters or their world isn't advanced a jot. The appearances of *Black Panther*'s superlative cast in these culminating movies feels more like a well-deserved victory lap than anything else, and that's fine by me.

And then there was the time T'Challa became Star-Lord of the Guardians of the Galaxy in Marvel's *What If...?* animated series (2021).

Had Chadwick Boseman not died, Black Panther's prominence in the Marvel Cinematic Universe would have been assured. He might even have become an occasional Avenger when he wasn't caring for Wakanda. Frankly, the character was on course to become more central to the MCU than he ever was to the comics universe. Boseman's absence, though, created a curious circumstance. *Black Panther* was a phenomenon, and Boseman's performance was obviously a large catalyst for that. It's not yet clear how Marvel will handle the issue of a replacement Panther; it probably won't be Shuri, though she could be considered next in line. We also know that it will be a different character—not T'Challa played by another actor (a thankless task—ask George Lazenby). But the phenomenon of *Black Panther* is bigger than Black Panther or the actor who plays him. People need to return to Wakanda, as they will in the sequel and the Coogler-produced *World of Wakanda* TV project.

Boseman's charisma brought people into the world of *Black Panther*, but now that world (and our world) will have to exist without him—appropriately, someone will inherit the role. *Black Panther: Wakanda Forever* promises to be more strongly tied to the Marvel Cinematic Universe—it's said to include such characters as Namor, the Sub-Mariner, the ruler of Atlantis (that's all the same guy) and Ironheart, a feisty, young, Black, female, self-made Iron Man. Would it have taken the same turn had Boseman not died (*What If...*)? Probably—Marvel has become very good at playing the long game—but I'm thankful that *Black Panther* will always stand on its own.

*Black Panther* becomes more consequential than most Marvel movies through its Black hero and African setting. It's *cool* that the world knows that Tony Stark, millionaire industrialist, is Iron Man; it *matters* that the world knows or will know that Black Panther is a Black man, and that he leads a super-advanced African nation. It *matters* that Killmonger is not just a ne'er-do-well like Loki, lusting for power for its own sake, because while he might be fictional like Loki, he brings with him a politics that belongs to our world. The implications of his rise or fall matter, the response of others to what he espouses matters, his giving voice to the conditions under which two billion people live ... matters.[71]

The ambivalence of popular culture rears its head: *Black Panther* could be understood as transcending the tropes of its genre to become something greater, or it might be compromised and limited by the demands of a genre that dictate the dichotomous binaries of heroes and villains. The final confrontation between T'Challa and Killmonger presents two nearly identical figures duking it out in a decent fight scene, but what does it have to do with the politics of Wakanda? The nature of the battle is separate from the political conflict; really, it could be *any* two guys in catsuits scrapping away. Or is that the point? One can admire the mano a mano nature of the duel, so different from the alien invasions and CGI spectacles that climax nearly every other superhero movie, or be frustrated by the reduction of an ideological conflict to a "cool fight scene." Whatever, it's a superhero movie, and it has to end with a fight. But does this battle even begin to blunt the power of this profoundly steeped-in-Blackness blockbuster?

# Black Panther's Black Body

Writing in the early 1990s about Black entertainment, Cornel West and Stuart Hall each considered the intellectual shift in the later twentieth century away from the cultural hegemony of white, Eurocentric thought and artistic production, the shift "from high culture to American mainstream popular culture and its mass-cultural, image-mediated, technological forms."[1] Hall writes of Black (indeed all) popular culture in terms that recall Richard Dyer's: it "is not at all, as we sometimes think of it, the arena where we find who we really are, the truth of our experience. It is an arena that is profoundly mythic. It is a theater of popular desires, a theater of popular fantasies."[2] Those fantasies need not be utopian, although they can be. Popular culture is a repository of "alternative traditions . . . counterposed to elite or high culture" (aesthetically and intellectually).[3] The creative arenas of music, literature, street art, filmmaking, and comics were less policed by such gated institutions as museums, endowments, and academia, and as a consequence popular cultures, including a vibrant Black popular culture, flourished.

The general shift was fortuitous for scholars like me, happily dissertating about science fiction literature, movies, and comics under the sign of postmodernism, but the gradual legitimation of swathes of Black cultural work, through the scholarship that began to accompany it, was huge, with far-reaching implications. The cultural politics that West, Hall, and others identified was rooted in an attention to cultural difference with the power, as Hall put it, "to trash the monolithic and homogeneous in the name of diversity, multiplicity, and heterogeneity," something that accelerated around the impact of civil rights and decolonization on Black diasporic peoples.[4] All this allowed the belated acknowledgment and appreciation of Black contributions to popular culture by elite institutions. In the world of superheroes an increasingly diverse coterie of writers, artists, editors, and directors could gain both employment and recognition as they shepherded superheroes of different races, nationalities, sexual orientations, genders, or levels of ability into being.

Black experience might be objectified and commodified in popular culture; it might be "deformed, incorporated, and unauthentic." Nevertheless, Hall proposes that "we continue to see, in the figures and the repertoires on which popular culture draws, the experiences that stand behind them."[5] Hall underscores the foregrounding of the Black body within popular forms (he refers to music, but movies and sports also work), which proliferates as a site of meaning "as if it was, and it often was, the only cultural capital we had. We have worked on ourselves as the canvases of representation."[6] As discussed, the superhero body has also served as a site of meaning, and so this chapter will concentrate on the intersectional "canvas" of Black Panther's Black body.

Black Panther is not just another superhero who happens to be Black. Blackness is fundamental to both the character's and the movie's power.

But before we go on, we should at least briefly ask: Is *Black Panther* a work of Black popular culture at all? It's a production of Marvel Studios, a subsidiary of the Disney Corporation, for goodness' sake, from comic book source material created by Jewish Americans. But when a film is written, directed, and designed (production and costumes) by creators of color, and when the director's other films have been dedicated to the presentation of Black life and lives, and when it highlights Black actors and African culture almost exclusively, it would seem to me to fit the bill.[7] Carvell Wallace admits that *Black Panther*'s status as a Hollywood movie about a fantasy nation could be a problem, but coming "from a director like Coogler, [it] must also function as a place for multiple generations of Black Americans to store some of our most deeply held aspirations."[8] Popular culture, after all, is rarely "pure"; Hall refers to its "contradictory, hybrid spaces."[9] One thing is for sure: the movie was received by Black audiences as a work of Black art, on a scale and to a degree that it would be churlish to contest.[10]

When *Wonder Woman*, *Black Panther*, and *Captain Marvel* came out, when Obama became president, when Kamala Harris—not just a woman but a woman of color—became vice president, or whenever some heretofore white male bastion is opened to something more inclusive, there's a phrase that's become ubiquitous: *The hero looks like me.*[11] The words couldn't be more matter-of-fact, but the tone holds a note of wonder. That hero—*that* one—up there on the screen? That hero looks like *me.*

At first glance, there's not much to analyze. The statement implicitly and explicitly makes a single point: that at last, finally, I, or my community, or—perhaps most important—my child has been included, been granted a seat at the table, been made to feel welcome, even significant. The figure on the screen models behaviors and values with which I/we can identify; they provide models to which I/we can aspire. In ways both incremental and monumental, the world has become just that much more inclusive. Children can imagine new possibilities for the future; they might even imagine themselves superheroes.

Consider Frantz Fanon's experience of the comics of an earlier day:

> The Tarzan stories, the sagas of twelve-year-old explorers, the adventures of Mickey Mouse, and all those "comic books" serve actually as a release for collective aggression. The magazines are put together by white men for little white men. This is the heart of the problem. In the Antilles—and there is every reason to think that the situation is the same in the other colonies—these same magazines are devoured by the local children. In the magazines the Wolf, the Devil, the Evil Spirit, the Bad Man, the Savage are always symbolized by Negroes or Indians; since there is always identification with the victor, the little Negro, quite as easily as the little white boy, becomes an explorer, an adventurer, a missionary "who faces the danger of being eaten by the wicked Negroes." I shall be told that this is hardly important; but only because those who say it have not given much thought to the role of such magazines.[12]

The only available site of identification for the "little Negro" of the colonies is the victor, who is also their own oppressor.

There were those who, from pretty early on, created more

diverse comics characters precisely to exert a more positive or uplifting influence. Wonder Woman, designed by William Moulton Marston to provide a role model for girls built upon strength and independence, made her first appearance in the pages of *Sensation Comics* in 1941.[13] African American publisher Orrin C. Evans established *All-Negro Comics* in 1947 to feature Black characters in a range of roles, from dramatic to comedic, to—in the person of Lion Man—superheroic. The comic barely made it onto newsstands.[14] The superhero revival in the 1960s coincided with the increasingly visible struggles for Black and women's rights, which encouraged Marvel and DC to diversify their rosters, an impulse that has waxed and waned with the years. There was the wave of Black urban superheroes in the 1970s and, more recently, attempts to recast so-called legacy heroes (the big guns—Superman, the Flash, Spider-Man) with non-white male alternatives: at Marvel, Miles Morales (Spider-Man) in 2011, Kamala Khan (Ms. Marvel) in 2014, Jane Foster (as that most masculine of heroes, Thor) also in 2014, and myriad others. DC and other publishers made their own moves. DC's rebooted Batwoman was a lesbian, and its introduction of John Stewart—a Black Green Lantern—may well have been, in 1971, the first such recasting (though he was *literally* a backup Lantern).

Some of this was market driven. Putting a Black kid front and center on the cover of *Spider-Man* could generate buzz and pull in a demographic less enthralled by the escapades of some half-century-old super-geezer. And besides, Peter Parker, the "Amazing" Spider-Man, wasn't going anywhere: Morales was the "Ultimate" Spider-Man in a whole different universe, taking up the Spider-mantle after the death of *that* universe's Peter Parker. Nevertheless, when Brian Michael Bendis introduced Morales in 2011, a portion of fandom was, um, aggrieved. *Why kill* [a version of] *Peter Parker? Why replace him with an Afro-Latino? Political correctness! A publicity stunt at the expense of the True Fans!* (Wanna see "white fragility" in action? Make a Black Spider-Man.)[15]

I didn't really have a dog in the Spider-Man fight, but I did wonder why, beyond the hype, Marvel didn't just introduce Miles as a brand-new superhero—what, did they run out of superpowers? But making Miles Spider-Man immediately shone a big ol' spotlight on the issue of whiteness in superhero comics. As Bendis pointed out—in what became the central trope of *Spider-Man: Into the Spider-Verse*—*anyone* can wear the mask; for all the world knows, the head-to-toe-garbed Spider-Man could have been non-white all along.[16] But it's easy to introduce diverse characters to the comics, and more difficult to sell them. Making Morales the new Spidey made a statement: the world changes. Get over it. Or, as Alexandra Petri puts it in a *Washington Post* headline, "The Response to the Black Spiderman [*sic*] Shows Why We Need One."[17] This tinkering with legacy heroes has become unremarkable (but for that self-same cohort threatened by any gesture of inclusivity), partly because it's more common (yay!) but also because it's often impermanent (boo!). Marvel has generally tried to have it both ways: green-lighting, to great fanfare, diversely populated hero projects (Coates's *Black Panther*, for example), then pulling the plug when sales inevitably flag.[18]

Petri, whose writing I generally admire, advocates for a kind of color-blind reading: "It seems to be a widespread belief among the makers and buyers of toys that people only go in for the Ones That Look Like Me.... Gay, straight, white, black, just tell us a good story. Please." Frankly, I approve of the superheroic affirmative action program, but I also think something more is going on there—something that has to do with superheroes as utopian, and their uniquely powerful ways of inhabiting space, world, and bodies.

Ta-Nehisi Coates's *Between the World and Me*, an essay that takes the form of a letter to his son, has at its center the vulnerability of the Black male body in the American "galaxy."[19] Given his subsequent stint as the writer of the *Black Panther* comic book, a turn to Coates is irresistible. The scholar and critic Osvaldo Oyola has considered the overlap, connecting the way Coates's collegiate self was disabused of his enchantment with the noble perfection of Black people ("kings in exile") to T'Challa's struggle to reassert his legitimacy as king of Wakanda. "This idealized land of kings," he writes, "is not as stable as the legends would have us think."[20]

But there's a more utopian overlap between Coates's essay and his *Black Panther* comics, located in his obsessive attention, in *Between the World and Me*, to the vulnerability and subjugation of the Black body.[21] The body is variously *confined, fragile, breakable, destroyed, shackled, erased, shattered, contorted, beaten, raped, robbed,* and *pillaged*.

None of this is going to happen to the body of Black Panther.[22]

"In America," Coates writes, "it is tradition to destroy the black body—it is heritage."[23] His mission is to contextualize and hammer home this brutal history for his son, who's experienced less of it firsthand. The Black body Coates describes—"a body more fragile than any other in this country"—is a body at mortal risk of destruction; American culture confers "the right to beat, rape, rob, and pillage the black body."[24] This catalog of horrors that can be (and has been) visited upon the Black body reads like the Negative Zone version of superhero bodies that fly, bend steel, turn invisible, and become gigantic—all those things that idealized, un-raced super-bodies can just *do*.

Less overtly brutal but no less egregious stratagems of everyday dehumanization are addressed in phenomenological writings by Charles Johnson and Iris Marion Young. Johnson emphasizes the Black male body while Young analyzes women's occupation of space; their texts overlap meaningfully in ways useful to parsing the significance of superhero bodies.[25] Black and female bodies are discussed as objects that are *looked at* in ways that constrain or negate the emergence of a fully functioning subjectivity.

Black subjectivity, for Fanon and others, is "overdetermined from without."[26] We are always an Other to another's gaze, Sartre tells us, but that relationship is not automatically one of abjection, as it is for Fanon: "I came into the world imbued with the will to find a meaning in things, my spirit filled with the desire to attain to the source of the world, and then I found that I was an object in the midst of other objects."[27] Johnson elaborates: "It is from whites that the intention, the 'meaning' of the black body comes."[28]

There is an analogous condition for women defined through male gazes and expectations. Young defines "feminine bodily existence" as "an inhibited intentionality," forever living the contradiction between the "I can" of embodied engagement with the world and a defensive "I cannot" that results from a double objectification: "the threat of being seen" *plus* "the threat of invasion of her body space."[29] Inhibited intent translates into inhibitions on action. And so you *learn* to stop trusting your body, to hold it all in, to reduce your visibility, to "throw like a girl."

Objectified by the outside gazes of misogyny and racism, all too conscious of how they're seen before they even see themselves, women and Black men cannot fully inhabit their own positions in the world. Women and African Americans were the two earliest groups demanding diversity from the world of superheroes: Young and Johnson make clear the phenomenological, as well as the political, imperatives behind those demands.

The quest for role models that "look like me" is a quest for strong characters: women who are more than romantic interests, homemakers, or home destroyers; minoritarian characters with agency who aren't subservient to white systems of power. "Strong," in these cases, refers more to *moral* than physical strength; when physical power is valued, it's generally a manifestation of moral strength.

But I think it's possible to skip the "moral" part and still have something to identify with: a *corporeal* rather than a moral identification. Such blaxploitation heroes as Superfly and *Black Caesar*'s Tommy Gibbs aren't the most morally admirable characters in moviedom, but one can't help but identify with the way they look and move, the way they occupy space—all their insurgent transgressions.[30] At least some part of Killmonger's undeniable appeal in *Black Panther* is simply the mesmerizing physicality of Michael B. Jordan.

There's more at stake—*even* more at stake—than "balanced" representation and moral positivity in the intersection of Black (and Other) bodies with superhero bodies. There's also the ability to display *power* in what might seem like the least radical of terms: the power to be *seen*, to be seen as you *choose* to be, the power to *fight*, the power to fight *back*, the power to *imagine* alternative ways of being and *embody* new ways of belonging in the world.

For it isn't only about superheroes that "look like me"; the radicalism lies in the realization that not only are there heroes that look like me but *they're allowed to inhabit the world in ways I am not.*

Johnson and Young position Black male and white female subjects as *looked at* but not *seen* in ways that allow agency, intention, and action, or that allow them to be self-possessed subjects. Johnson writes, "My body gives me the world, but, as that world is given, it is one in which I can be unseen."[31] Superheroes, on the other hand, are unseen only when they so choose. Many have some kind of super-sight, but superhero-ism isn't just about super-seeing; it's about being super-seen. A flamboyant costume announces the superhero, even the ones who lurk among the shadows, making them visible to the world. Perhaps the true function of the secret identity is to allow this repeated blossoming of the superhero on the urban or world stage, to continually replay the shift from unseen to seen and back again. The costumes are supposedly meant to strike fear in the hearts of superstitious criminals, but, let's face it, they're a tactic of display.

A secret identity is no longer de rigueur for the modern superhero. No longer can consumers of superhero fiction imagine themselves as secret Supermans; no longer do the stories turn on so many Lois Lanes out to prove Superman and Clark are one and the same. No longer do superheroes have day jobs, whether as photojournalists or test pilots. The only remaining persona is the public one, the only self the one on display, the one that is seen, the one whose exceptionalism is worn, as it were, on one's sleeve.

Black heroes were in the vanguard of the secret-less approach to superherodom. Luke Cage wrapped himself in a canary yellow top, a silver tiara, and a (bit on-the-nose) length of heavy chain for a belt, but it never even occurred to him to mask up. Black Lightning was masked (and Afro-wigged) to project more of a "street" vibe than the middle-class high school teacher/principal he was. But John Stewart, Earth's new second-string Green Lantern, was having none of it; he liked his snazzy new uniform, but: "Only one thing . . . I won't wear any **mask**! This black man lets it **all** hang out! I've got **nothing** to hide!"[32]

This feels interesting to me: the white superhero's devotion to secret identities spoke to fantasies of hidden depths beneath a drab exterior, but, regardless, the gainfully employed, upstanding white citizen that was Clark Kent was doing fine; he could afford the luxury of anonymity. To be unseen was a private joke between him and the (Superman-wannabe or could've-been) comics reader—Clark's biggest problem was that Lois liked Superman better (*chuckle*).[33]

For the Black superhero, being unseen is no joke—it's nothing less than the condition of being itself, falling just this side of erasure.

The Black superhero's rejection of the mask goes well beyond a defiance of genre convention: Black people in America are masked almost by definition. In Paul Laurence Dunbar's 1895 poem "We Wear the Mask," the mask is the false face presented to white culture: "We wear the mask that grins and lies," it begins. "Why should the world be over-wise / In counting all our tears and sighs? / Nay, let them only see us, while / We wear the mask."[34] To wear the mask is to fly below the radar, to take on a position of invisibility—being visible comes at great cost. Small wonder that Black superheroes choose to announce their identity, loud and proud, without equivocation or prevarication or masks. Luke Cage even hands out business cards.

Black Panther, though, wasn't introduced as a superhero with a superhero's mission, but as someone who just so happened to have a "stalking costume" that couldn't help but signal superhero or supervillain. Not until he joins the Avengers does he become a proper superhero—fulfilling, in a sense, the destiny of the costume. And it's during his stint as an Avenger that he takes on that secret identity as an inner-city school teacher. Many a Panther writer has, in effect, tamed the beast that is Black Panther, turning down the volume on the qualities that make him unique to better fit the template Ramzi Fawaz identified of the African American urban superhero.[35] The movie will have none of this; *Black Panther*'s version of T'Challa is joyously Wakandan and gloriously a king. Being a superhero is so *ordinary*.

In the pages of *Fantastic Four*, Black Panther's garb was a solid black bodysuit (with cowl and cape) that covered his face. But there was clearly some editorial worrying around the edges at Marvel, revealed by the Panther's changing costume in the first years—the question being whether or not to show his dark skin. An earlier design exposed the lower part of the hero's face (à la Batman), and some later iterations return to that concept, including one early version of the movie costume.[36] In the history of superheroes, there have been a host of heroes and villains sporting a "Black" moniker—Black Terror, Black Adam, Black Canary, Black Widow—but none of them were actually *Black*. To entirely hide his skin might have the effect of downplaying race; the Panther's racial Blackness could be an occasional encounter rather than a constant presence.[37] But the full-body version has its own irresistible power. Alex Szeptycki points out that since "his costume bears no signifier"—no logo, no text—"the literal blackness of his costume becomes the main signifier of his identity."[38] T'Challa's individual race is subsumed by the symbolic power of race itself.

*The half-mask.* Fantastic Four, *vol. 1, no. 52 (July 1966).*
*Unused cover. Jack Kirby (pencils), Joe Sinnott (inks).*

The argument as to which might be the more racially progressive costume can spin either way; there's no singular "right" approach. There's that messy popular culture again—what reads as subversive *here* comes off as reactionary *there*—but this messiness can be generative for consumers and producers alike.

*The beast that is Black Panther.* Discourses of objectification and dehumanization intersect with long-standing associations of dark-skinned Africans (and descendent African Americans) with "animals," associations that are, shall we say, less celebratory than one finds in *Black Panther.* White discourse has continually produced "black(ened) animality as abjection," in the words of Zakiyyah Iman Jackson.[39] Charles Johnson writes that "to black subjectivity is attributed the contents that white consciousness itself fears to contain or confront: bestial sexuality, uncleanliness, criminality, all the purported 'dark things.'"[40] Johnson finds early twentieth-century writings, including books like *The Leopard's Spots* by the infamous Thomas Dixon Jr. (of *The Clansman* fame) to be replete with fearful animal analogies that cast Blacks as subhuman, incapable of transcending their bestial "natures," unfit to intermingle with white folk. He writes that Black blood carries with it "the germ of the underworld and the traits of lower orders of animals." The light-skinned and those of mixed race are especially pernicious because of their ability to pass; they only *appear* "unstained."[41] Many is the reference to "the Negro beast." Jackson argues, "Slavery, in particular the slave narrative, established the terms through which we commonly understand the bestialization of blackness"—dehumanization was instrumental in sustaining the institution.[42] Recall Fanon's colonialist child, reading tales of Tarzan of the Apes, the Wolf, and the Savage.

The superhero's alignment with animality skews more broadly. From the first appearance of "the Bat-Man" in early 1939, superheroes and villains have continually and reliably drawn their iconography and powers from the animal kingdom, both wild and domestic: scorpions, black widows, lions, ants, crocodiles, Howard the Duck—the list goes on.[43] Animal Man gains the powers of any animal around him; Beast Boy turns into green ones. And it's not racialized: Batman was/is a white billionaire, and the first Spider-Man was a white kid from Queens. Women are associated with animals as much as men (all too often as felines), and the same is true for superheroes of Otherness. The lesbian incarnation of Batwoman, after all, has the same totem as her straight male counterpart.

When animality intersects abjection, it's overwhelmingly among villains (and a few mutant heroes only sometimes coded as animal—Beast, Wolverine). Marvel had a near lock on these: Spider-Man alone fought the Lizard, the Rhino, the Scorpion, two versions of the Vulture, and, lest we forget, Doctor Octopus.

But in the world of super*heroes*, animal/human intersectionality isn't a negative articulation. It ties into animistic folkloric and religious systems—including from Africa—predicated upon respectful relations to the animal world, to say nothing of the joys of dress-up. As Blair Davis points out, "The decision to call the first black superhero 'Lion Man'... equates the hero with power, nobility and majesty."[44] Superheroes partake of the regality of the lion, the proportionate strength of the spider, the nocturnal habits of the bat (and its ability to trigger fear), the unerring vision of the hawk, the stealth of the cat, the size of the ant, and the whatever of the robin—in every case, a positive hybridization of human and animal. Our Black Panther has plenty of company.[45]

Superheroes might even belong to a category of production, privileged by Jackson, that "creatively disrupt[s] the human-animal distinction and its persistent raciality . . . providing unruly yet generative conceptions of being."[46] Such "alternative conceptions of being and the nonhuman" can destabilize persistent and restrictive racist binaries.[47] Even before considering race, superheroes *already* embody "unruly yet generative" ways of being in the world; in the hands of thoughtful creators and readers, these creative disruptions can be quite resonant.

But Jackson is nearly as suspicious of *super*humans as *sub*humans. Black(ened) people "are cast as sub, supra, and human simultaneously," creating pressures to be, at once, "everything and nothing."[48] In the trial of George Floyd's murderer, one of Derek Chauvin's attorneys argued that his actions were "reasonable" because Floyd was resisting arrest with drug-related "superhuman strength." Floyd was cast as the negative version of the superhuman—uncontrolled and uncontrollable, bestial, a conflation of supra- and sub-, but not *human*. It fell to the prosecutor, Steve Schleicher, to rebut: "There was no superhuman strength that day. There's no superhuman strength because there's no such thing as a superhuman. Those exist in comic books. . . . Just a human, just a man lying on the pavement, being pressed upon, desperately crying out—a grown man crying out for his mother, a human being."[49]

If culture is going to give us creatively disruptive super-bodies, then those bodies had better move well beyond

the categories of white, male, and straight. Black Panther—
created, remember, by white guys—could so easily have become part of the history of Black-as-beast. When the Fantastic
Four arrive in Wakanda, he immediately attacks: "I neglected
to tell you one thing—It is *you* who shall be hunted!" Another
day, another bestial predator. But, no! After eleven pages of a
perfectly entertaining superhero slugfest, the Panther reveals
that he's seeking allies, not prey. And, as even the Thing can
see, he's *very* civilized.

The shamanistic function of the Panther's mask and costume is explicit: Black Panther is a hereditary role celebrating
Bast, the Panther Goddess. "My mask is not for concealment—
but rather a symbol of my **Panther Power**!" The stalking
costume was designed for hunting prey rather than right-
ing wrongs and had nothing at all to do with disguise: all of
Wakanda knows that its king assumes this ritualistic garb.
The costume simultaneously highlights and hides: early in
the movie, T'Challa and Okoye need to extract Nakia from a
stealth mission she's running against human traffickers. They
come in quiet, but their targets are suspicious, edgy. A startled
dog barks at something up a tree. A trafficker's flashlight beam
follows its gaze to reveal Black Panther in an iconic pose:
crouched like his namesake upon a branch, ready to pounce.
The camera holds briefly; the scene erupts into fragmented
violence, the only light sources the muzzle flashes that reveal
the Panther in fleeting glimpses. Still something of a stalking
costume, it's also a singular assertion of identity and most *defi-
nitely* a superhero costume.

In the world of superheroes, Scott Jeffery posits "Animal
bodies" ("that from which the human came") at the opposite
pole from "Artificial bodies" ("that which comes after").[50]

Superheroic transformations usually enhance an essential humanity, but Jeffrey notes the anxieties that exist around degeneration, as with the devolution of the X-Men's Beast and such "monstrous (in)versions" as the one between Batman (more man than bat) and his tragic foe Man-Bat (more bat than man).[51] Superhero animality more typically positions the human in a less fraught relation to some sort of other-than-human, working, in its small way, against the fixity of human definition, perhaps even anthropocentric thought.

It's worth pointing out that superheroes of color are rarely aligned with abjection; it's mutants who seem the most abject. On the other hand, if the X-Men have served more or less openly as allegorical Others (Black, queer, Jewish), then perhaps abjection and Blackness are aligned, if obliquely. But *actually* Black superheroes—powerful and self-determining—are more likely to be pressed into service as (Poitier-like) "positive" or even "uplifting" avatars of Black pride than as avatars of abjection. So, *allegorically* Other heroes are frequently abject figures while *explicitly* racialized heroes are allowed transcendent power. Huh.

Johnson discusses a human-animal conflation that one senses he's encountered *a lot*—a white basketball fan praises Walt Frazier in itchily familiar terms: "He moves like—like a cheetah, or a big jungle cat."[52] The guy might mean well, but history is embedded in such language. It's entirely possible that Lee and Kirby were pulling a "Walt Frazier" in presenting a laudatory African character with some condescension, but this particular "Negro beast" is nevertheless both a king and a technological genius. Their promising template will be taken up and expanded upon by later writers, both white and Black. The stalking costume will take on folkloric and talismanic associations, while Wakanda's history as an unconquered, advanced nation will gain a talismanic power of its own. Black Panther himself will be positioned as the African analog to Captain America—the moral center of the Marvel Universe.

Denotatively and connotatively, what is most emphatically signaled by Black Panther's costume is *Blackness*, a Blackness both corporeal (the Black body) and conceptual (think of "darkest" Africa). It is Blackness redoubled—the black of the costume and the dark skin beneath it—laying claim to its value and place in the world. It refuses the purported "dark things" of racist assumption even as it embraces a totemistic and ennobling, but still powerful, animality.[53]

The colonizing gaze is ineffective against this Black body and this nation; it has been rejected. The system no longer controls what is seen and unseen. Wakanda hides, but it will re-emerge when the time is right; the Panther displays in self-defined ways that speak to who he is as well as the traditions he follows. It is they who control what others see and know, and what stories they tell. "The symbol of the black body . . . if interrogated, should disclose a racial experience wrought mythically," writes Charles Johnson—something true, even if it isn't exactly what he had in mind, of Black Panther.[54]

Fascinating though superheroes may be, they hardly represent the first or even the primary(!) medium through which Black persons and communities controlled the ways they were seen. Amateur and studio photography in the twentieth century could not only ignore stereotypes and the view "from without," but at the same time catalog alternative modes of self-presentation. Pointing to both the centrality and the importance of photography, bell hooks wrote, "Cameras gave to black folks, irrespective of our class, a means by which we could participate fully in the production of images," creating, in the end, "a counter-hegemonic world of images that would stand as visual resistance."[55]

W. E. B. Du Bois's curated collection of photographs, exhibited at the American Negro Exhibit at the 1900 Paris Exposition, emphasized the breadth of Black physiognomies, skin tones, and social positions, challenging the long legacies of racist taxonomies in such photographic "archives" as lynching images, ethnographic studies, and "scientific" catalogs of the "Negro type." This "counterarchive," as Shawn Michelle Smith calls it, offers "a place from which a counter-history can be imagined and narrated."[56] The image of Black Americans was no longer filtered only through the literal and conceptual lenses of white photographers; the exhibit as a whole insisted upon—and instantiated—"an African American presence in the face of the spectacular erasures produced by lynching."[57]

*Black Panther*'s cast is almost entirely Black, and one could claim it as its own counterarchive to the whiteness of the superhero genre and Hollywood film generally. It didn't have to be this way—the movie could have been set in America with a small supporting cast of Wakandans. It could have featured a more racially "balanced" cast (throw in a couple of Avengers at the very least). But no. The nearly all-Black cast insists on and instantiates a jubilant contestatory image, here staged in the arena of the multiplex rather than a world exposition.

The snapshot, for hooks, served to articulate African American self-images, presenting "ordinary" lives made visible on their own terms. Through this implicitly "oppositional subculture," she writes, "dehumanization could be countered."[58] The movie camera is a camera, too, and Black filmmaking is all about controlling the image. A film like the neo-neo-realist *Killer of Sheep*, directed and shot by Charles Burnett (1973), highlights and preserves something of the domestic milieu and everyday life that hooks celebrates in amateur photography of local people and places.

But the camera can do more than document the real: the glossier world of studio photography also contributes to the counterarchive. Deborah Willis's *Posing Beauty* exhibition catalog takes up a quote from Ben Arogundade, the author of *Black Beauty* (2000), and offers it as something of a manifesto: "The right to be beautiful and to be acknowledged as such wherever you are, wherever you are from is not so much a folly as a human-rights issue. In writing the history of the black experience did we forget something important? Did we forget about beauty?"[59] The exhibition tracks the history of Black men and women using photography "to experiment with varied ideas of themselves and ultimately to honor how they saw themselves and wished to be seen by others." For their subjects and participants, studio photography and beauty contests established "spaces where they could express their desired selves."[60]

The camera in Black life became an implicit political instrument, producing forms of what hooks calls "visual resistance," but she expresses regret that more overtly political "black freedom movements were often only concerned with questions of 'good' and 'bad' imagery," promoting "notions of essence and identity that ultimately restricted and confined black image production."[61] A photographic practice rooted in posing, play-acting, and fantasy could be positively disruptive to the stability of categories, including political categories, challenging the singularity of Black "experience" and definition. The studio where Ryan Coogler made *Black Panther* may operate on an altogether different scale than one operated by a local Black portrait photographer, or even the studio used by a fashion photographer preparing a glamorous photo shoot for *Essence*, but it, too, makes its own contribution to the counterarchive of alternative images, which I'll discuss in a second.

Photography, for hooks, provided "a sense of how [they] looked when [they] were not 'wearing the mask,'" but there's something to be said for the parallel importance of *choosing* a mask.[62] It could be a pose or a hairstyle; it could be the ornately playful garb of Sun Ra, Isaac Hayes, Prince, Grace Jones, Janelle Monáe, or the whole P-Funk mob. It could be a vibranium-threaded nanotechnological Black Panther mask. Superheroes have always been flamboyant assertions of self; the self-defined and self-presenting Black superhero is just a little more in-your-face about it.

One last photograph to consider: Christopher Freeburg's *Black Aesthetics and the Interior Life* features a single image—a photograph of a man named Frank Embree standing tall just before his lynching on July 22, 1899. The photo demands that we try to "read" him—his expression, his posture, his attitude—to see and understand, to empathize with what we think we know. But Freeburg recasts this image, pointing out that it is, in the end, opaque. There's a lot we might *like* to see there, or even *believe* we see: pride, defiance, dignity (or anxiety, fear, horror); but this image does not give up this man's secrets. Freeburg is fascinated by such "unknowability," caesurae that reveal that there is more to "Black experience" and identity than can be expressed publicly and politically. Moreover, not all experiences of Black people are reducible to *a* or *the* Black experience:

> By reading the horizon of racial conflict and black aesthetics solely in terms of black collective politics, we miss something that equally defines it: ongoing moments

where black artists repeatedly invoke and dramatize
questions like who am I, what do I value, where do I find
community and how the answers to these questions are
so often ambiguous, enigmatic, or withheld entirely.[63]

Read through Freeburg, Embree's image has value for what it
conceals and deflects, rather than what it (perhaps) reveals.
Embree's interiority is unknown and will forever remain unknown. The unreadability of his image makes it unsuitable
as a lynching postcard; the images taken after his death are
safer, predictable and singular in their meaning. In its very
opacity, though, the image of Embree standing, whipped and
wounded, on his own feet, has a place in the photographic
counterarchive of resistance.

The true site of unknowability in *Black Panther*, as I'll
argue later, is Erik Killmonger. Here, I'm interested in Freeburg's focus on aspects of experience that are not so easily
read through the lens of Black collective politics, that unsettle
settled categories, and that might even connect to Arogundade's question regarding beauty: "In writing the history of the
black experience did we forget something important?"

The outrageousness of Bootsy or Grace Jones, the opacity
of Frank Embree, and the costume of Black Panther all have
the effect of seizing control of the narrative, of generating (or
refusing) meaning on one's own terms, and of negating the
gazes that might seek to contain and neuter the presence one
chooses to project into the world.

*Black Panther*, as I claimed earlier, makes its contribution
to the counterarchive. And to spend so much of this chapter on the abjection of the Black body without considering

its beauty would be just plain wrong. Chadwick Boseman, to take but one actor in *Black Panther*, is not only beautiful but presented as such. All the "alternative images" just discussed, these self-imaginings and self-presentations, even Embree's ambiguous posture, allow me to more thoroughly understand what is, for me, the movie's most powerful moment—when Black Panther, presumed to have been killed in his challenge duel with Killmonger, reappears.

Fighters loaded with vibranium weapons are beginning to fly, carrying their destructive might to aid in Killmonger's mission of Black global liberation. One abruptly crashes, and as Killmonger and his troops watch, Black Panther, costumed and masked, emerges from the flames to stand, resurrected, atop the wreckage. The camera tracks toward him as choral voices and horns crescendo (they sing "ukumkani wethu"— "our king" in Xhosa[64]). His nanotech helmet dissolves to show us the face of T'Challa. "N'Jadaka!" he yells, beginning to walk toward Killmonger, who, looking cocky but uncertain, answers with a "Whassup?" The Panther's theme music emerges on the soundtrack. Okoye is radiant: "He lives!"

Framed from the waist up, wearing a look of fierce determination we've not seen before, T'Challa calls out, "I never yielded!" He spreads his arms wide—to the very edges of this very wide screen—and as he says the next line, a small but proud smile plays across his face and a light comes into his eyes: "And as you can see, I am *not* dead!" It's difficult to avoid thinking him Christ-like when seeing him reborn, arms stretched and backed by a chorus of angels, but I see neither martyr nor savior. I see a Black man reclaiming his broken body and asserting its integrity, facing the one who would destroy it, proclaiming his presence and his right not to the throne, but to simply and defiantly *exist*. His outstretched arms offer himself (his self) as a demonstrable and irrefutable fact, the form-fitting black costume with its purple traceries of force and muscle underscoring and signaling the blackness of his body.

*"I never yielded!"*

Up to the moment of writing this, I thought the important part of his declaration was "I am *not* dead." Now I understand that it's really "As you can *see*."

One of the things we can see, and can see only more clearly since his death, is the beauty of Chadwick Boseman, animated, vibrant, gorgeous, and joyous before us. "I never yielded," he says. "And I am *not* dead."

The face of T'Challa is also the face of Chadwick Boseman—when the helmet dissolves we see both at once. Both at once is often how I watch movies, simultaneously invested in character and actor. I occupy two viewing positions and find nothing at all paradoxical in that. But, following his death, in this moment I now see Boseman more than the Panther. Below his face his body is lithe and supple, an effect accentuated by his body-hugging costume.

Boseman and Panther look entirely self-possessed, and I'm thrown back onto the regality of Chadwick Boseman, a regality that cut across nearly all his roles. Boseman played avatars of Black excellence, and his characters were confident in their abilities. "He's practically superhuman," someone says of him, and another calls him "a hero." They're not talking about Black Panther, though, but Jackie Robinson, number 42. Robinson, in *42* (Brian Helgeland, 2013), has no need to prove his athletic prowess to Branch Rickey; rather, he has to demonstrate that he can keep his cool in the face of sustained racist abuse (strong enough to *not* fight back, as Rickey tells him). Thurgood Marshall (*Marshall*) breezes into town to help win a landmark case, then heads off to wherever he's needed next, like Tom Joad with a law degree, or Shane, or Batman. The people welcome him as something of a savior; I expected someone to ask, "Who was that masked man? I wanted to thank him!" James Brown, in *Get On Up* (Tate Taylor, 2014), is convinced of his own genius before he even knows what he'll be a genius *at*; it turns out he can hear rhythms and orchestrations no one else can. And, of course, there's T'Challa.

In his achingly brief career, Boseman played a lot of superheroes. In Spike Lee's *Da 5 Bloods* (2020) he appears only in the Vietnam flashbacks, unaged, untouched, mythic. His surviving army buddies, now older, speak of him with reverence.

Levee (his final role, in *Ma Rainey's Black Bottom* [George C. Wolfe, 2020]) is seemingly a hotshot trumpeter on the cusp of getting his own band to play his own songs, a self-made man who knows how to stand up to the white man. To be anachronistic for a moment, he thinks he's Jackie Robinson, Thurgood Marshall, James Brown, and Black Panther all in one. In reality he's overeager and willfully blind to all the shucking and jiving he has to do for the white record producer who's about to steal his songs for five bucks apiece. He isn't what he thinks he is, and what he thinks he is is a Chadwick Boseman character.

But I have to say that as an actor, Boseman doesn't give much away. There's a wariness; he often looks at others sideways, as if suspecting that someone somewhere (or everyone everywhere) is going to try to put something past him. Wesley Snipes would have been a much hotter Black Panther (hot as in *runs hot*); Boseman keeps his cool.[65]

A confession: until the moment I learned of Boseman's death (and I know exactly where I was when my phone buzzed), I thought *Black Panther* was a Michael B. Jordan movie in disguise (more about him in the final chapter). Had Coogler been able to cast him as T'Challa, I thought, he would have (an unfounded speculation and undoubtedly wrong). Boseman I found comparatively unaffecting. Life is something of a struggle for most of Jordan's protagonists, while Boseman's T'Challa was to the manor born.

After he died, amid the expressions of grief from all corners of America and beyond, I belatedly recognized just how powerful an icon Boseman/T'Challa/Black Panther had become. I went back to focus more on his performance. And I found the regality, the confidence, and the grace (Richard Brody calls him "perhaps the most graceful [actor] of his generation"), but also the wariness, the guardedness, and the reserve.[66] *Black Panther* is filled with faces more animated than Boseman's, and animated faces draw attention (at least mine): Jordan, but also Gurira (Okoye), Wright (Shuri), Duke (M'Baku), and even the more minor characters played by Martin Freeman (Everett Ross) and Andy Serkis (Klaue).[67]

But what I took to be nothing but emotional reserve was

as much a *stillness* through which Boseman projected centeredness, stability, and self-possession.[68] His characters possess an inner strength so fundamental that they wouldn't even recognize the term (except for Levee, who hasn't any)—inner strength coupled with external beauty and a physical grace that manifests more in the way Boseman walks across a room than in anything he does in the guise of Black Panther (even if "Black Panther" *weren't* primarily a stunt performer aided by CGI effects). Check out the moment when he enters Shuri's lab—T'Challa is working some serious James Brown swagger.[69]

I return again (and again) to this: "I never yielded! And as you can see I am *not* dead." Arms flung wide, hint of a smile, light in his eyes. There's none of the hypermasculinity one might associate with superheroes or superstars. Like all live-action movie images, it's fictional (there is no Black Panther) and documentary (there was a Chadwick Boseman, in front of this camera, making that gesture, saying those lines). There is T'Challa in full possession of himself, no longer denying uncomfortable truths; there is Boseman in the full flower of his craft and stardom, owning the space of the screen and becoming every inch a superhero in the moment when his mask *dis*appears.[70]

Although the image, as I've presented it, has a kind of transparency, not the opacity that Freeburg located in the photograph of Embree, it's nevertheless (or has become) an image that invites speculation. Do we see Boseman behind T'Challa? Is he expressing what I say he is? I don't—*can't*—know. But as an image that fills the screen with the beauty of a Black man—as a superhero but also as himself—in order to do nothing more than announce and aver the existence of that man, it moves beyond the specific politics of the scene and the movie. Politics is part of it, but that doesn't nearly exhaust the experience of this moment.

*In writing the history of the black experience, did we forget something important? Did we forget about beauty?*

*Black Panther* did not.

To see in this an image of Black beauty is obviously to see more than Boseman's physical beauty, though there it is. It's to see an image of self-possession in the face of a potentially hostile world. An image of a Black artist by a Black artist. It announces the presence of T'Challa, of Boseman, of Coogler, of Black Panther, of *Black Panther*. Of Jackie Robinson, Thurgood Marshall, and James Brown—even Levee. And it's a synecdoche for all the images that make up *Black Panther*: Black bodies, sure, but also the costumes, adornments, families, dreams, and desires that surround and enworld those bodies. This image, these images, surely belong to that counterarchive.

Coates tells his son that America tries to "deny you and me the right to secure and govern our own bodies," and reminds him that his "beauty" is not separate from this history but "is largely the result of enjoying an abnormal amount of security in your black body."[71] I wonder what was the import, for Coates, of writing the adventures of the most abnormally "secure" Black body of all: a superhero, a king (*not* a king in exile).

"How do I live free in this black body?" Coates asks. "What would it be to act as though my body were my own?" He writes of "a cosmic injustice, a profound cruelty, which infused an abiding, irrepressible desire to unshackle" his body and "achieve the velocity of escape."[72]

Not so mysterious, then, that Coates seized the opportunity

to script a superhero comic, and while he says he wanted Spider-Man, Black Panther was a perfect match: a Black male body living free, unshackled, and not so easily erased. It is a Black male body that belongs to no one: "We are all our beautiful bodies and so must never be prostrate before barbarians, must never submit our original self, our one of one, to defiling and plunder."[73] Here Coates might as well be thinking of T'Challa, or of Wakanda.

He cautions his son to "resist . . . the comforting narrative of divine law, toward fairy tales that imply some irrepressible justice."[74] Those who resist fairy tales should probably steer clear of superheroes, but Coates's caution is directed toward the master-narratives and alternate histories that had once provided comfort (those "kings in exile"), not the Marvel comics he once enthusiastically read. In the 1970s and '80s, Marvel was "one of the few places you could see black heroes," Coates writes. "As a kid, I had comic books and hip-hop."[75]

Nothing wrong, then, with a little reparative fantasy, even a fairy tale or two.

As we'll see in the next chapters, some of *Black Panther*'s more radical critics have denigrated its fanciful Pan-Africanism, its homogenization of African diversity. But Jelani Cobb argues that "Wakanda is no more or less imaginary than the Africa conjured by Hume or Trevor-Roper, or the one canonized in such Hollywood offerings as 'Tarzan.' It is a redemptive counter-mythology."[76] Black Panther himself constitutes another counter-mythology—which is really the main argument of this chapter and this book. Coates's attention to the subjugation and destruction of Black bodies in the American "galaxy" seems to have summoned forth its fairy tale opposite: a corporeal countermyth.

Coates's *Black Panther* comics are not explicitly about the superhuman Black body—women and Wakandan society loom large in ways that influenced the movie—but its powerful corporeality is everywhere, figured through the visual imaginary of the comic and the trope of what Scott Jeffery calls the "perfect body" of the superhero.[77] If superheroes frame a liberatory imagination for Black and Other subjectivities, they do so, at the very least, by generating alternative ideas of what it is to be embodied in the world, to live different relations to power, and to possess bodies with the powers and abilities to define and redefine what is possible. In doing this, superheroes can indeed demonstrate "what utopia would feel like."

Utopia might involve a Black superhero whose body can resist the fate of so many Black Americans. Luke Cage, for example, has special abilities: "Bullets riddle his freakishly-transformed body, bruise it, but cannot **penetrate** it."[78] A bullet-proof Black man was a resonant enough metaphor in 1972, but translated to television in 2016, in the shadow of the shootings of Trayvon Martin, Michael Brown, Tamir Rice, Laquan McDonald, and so many others, it was *profound.* And beyond the power to stand up and fight, there is something to be said for the ability to fight *back*, to retaliate. The Black Panther costume designed by Shuri absorbs violent energy directed against it, visibly stores it, and turns it back on its source.[79]

The superhero is meant to be a selfless figure, with the costume a vehicle through which they do good.[80] But I've always seen something more gloriously egotistical: vibrantly expressive bodies and costumes as a singular and liberating form of self-declaration.[81] Here, in every bit of Black Panther's comportment and demeanor, we see exactly this: he stands and strides, costumed and unmasked, displaying himself to

*Panther power.*

the world, demanding to be *seen*. Black lives and Black bodies that won't be so easily ignored, shackled, or erased—this is what utopia might feel like.

Charles Johnson identifies three "modes of flight from the black as body situation," that condition of being defined from without. The first is to play the role of "empty" Black body, where, he writes, "not being acknowledged as a subject is my strength, my chance for cunning and masquerade, for guerrilla warfare."[82] It's a kind of secret identity ("We wear the mask"). The next involves performing against type: "I display my eloquence, culture, and my charm to demonstrate to the Other that I, despite my stained skin, do indeed have an inside."[83] Become a superhero of social uplift, a credit to the race.

"Or," he continues, "I am radical, and seize the situation at its root by reversing the negative meaning of the body and, therefore, the Black-as-body: 'It is beautiful, I say'...Meaning still derives from the white Other. I applaud my athletic, amorous, and dancing ability, my street-wisdom and savoir-faire, my 'soul.' "[84] Performed correctly, one can even position the white body as an impoverished version. There is a challenge to pulling off this configuration, however: "This persuasion in which stain and the black-as-body are inverted is ahistorical; it must involve a complete reconstitution of cultural meanings with the black body as its foundation: two thousand years of color and symbolism must be recast."[85]

That last one sounds big. It might even take more than a superhero to pull off. It might take a nation.

Welcome to Wakanda.

# The Wakandan Dream

The *New York Times* crossword puzzle for January 10, 2020, contained the following clue at 52 across: "*Black Panther* genre." Twelve letters. Hmmm. "SUPERHERO." No, only nine. Aha! "SCIENCEFICTION"! Uh-uh, fourteen. The answer, of course, was "AFROFUTURISM."[1]

Given that Black superheroes were foundational to the concept, Afrofuturism is a particularly appropriate lens through which to view *Black Panther*. Mark Dery coined the term in a brief piece published in 1993 as he wondered at the "perplexing" dearth of Black American science fiction writers—perplexing "in light of the fact that African Americans, in a very real sense, are the descendants of alien abductees; they inhabit a sci-fi nightmare in which unseen but no less impassable force fields of intolerance frustrate their movements."[2] He follows this bold analogy with another: "The sublegitimate status of science fiction as a pulp genre in Western literature mirrors the subaltern position to which blacks have been relegated."[3]

Two decades later, the science fiction/fantasy writer N. K. Jemisin underscored the same fundamental caesura haunting the genre in describing a negative epiphany she had while kicking back with *The Jetsons*:

> I notice something: there's nobody even slightly brown
> in the Jetsons' world. Even the family android sounds

white. This is supposed to be the real world's future, right? Albeit in silly, humorous form. Thing is,
not-white-people make up most of the world's population, now as well as back in the Sixties when the show
was created. So what happened to all those people, in
the minds of this show's creators? ... I'm watching the
*Jetsons*, and it's creeping me right the fuck out.[4]

Dery asked, "Can a community whose past has been deliber-
ately rubbed out, and whose energies have subsequently been
consumed by the search for legible traces of its history, imagine
possible futures?" He found affirmative answers across a swath
of Black popular media.[5] By casting a net that went beyond the
small circle of Black science fiction writers, formidable as they
were, Dery generated an expanded list of Afrofuturist creators,
contributors, and remixers "constellated from such far-flung
points" as the worlds of jazz, reggae, and funk; the visual art of
the street (including, as other critics did, album art and posters); the sounds and images of hip-hop; and the Black (and
Black-created) superheroes coming out of Milestone Comics
(Icon, Static, and the rest).[6]

Science fiction, in its most classic mode, is saddled with
the burden of at least *trying* to explicate how we arrive at its
various futures, analyzing and extrapolating from present situations to imagine not only change, but how change might
come to be. Other popular cultural forms are not so burdened.
Mark Sinker, writing around the same time as Dery, put it this
way: "The triumph of black American culture is that, forcibly
stripped by the Middle Passage and Slavery Days of any direct
connection with African mother culture, it has nonetheless
survived; by syncretism, by bricolage, by a day-to-day pro-

gramme of appropriation and adaptation as resourcefully broad-minded as any in history."[7] All Sun Ra, George Clinton, and Dwayne McDuffie (in his *Icon* comic book) had to do was rip off and riff off the energies of the present: "détourning," as the Situationists put it; or "willfully misusing," in Dery's words; or, as Zakiyyah Jackson has it, "creatively disrupting" the stuff of mainstream media to make it say or do *something else*.

Against the ongoing traumas of the history of enslaved peoples and the dangers of living modern life in America "while Black," the *something else* of Afrofuturism is almost axiomatically utopian, just as Richard Dyer framed it. Though responding to real social needs, entertainment doesn't present models of utopian worlds, as science fiction might be obligated to do; instead, "the utopianism is contained in the feelings it embodies."[8] To put it another way, Stuart Hall saw popular culture as a "profoundly mythic... theater of popular desires, a theater of popular fantasies."[9] While for Sinker, Black science fiction spun dystopically, taking place in a universe where "apocalypse already happened," *other* popular forms, with hip-hop at the forefront, included work that was "by turns grindingly bleak (as chroniclers of the present) and deliriously optimistic (as harbingers of the future)."[10]

Afrofuturist entertainment is also utopian in its profligate liberatory strategies and energies, its possible futures often predicated (explicitly or not) upon alternative histories, its practitioners repurposing existent culture to their own ends, building and unleashing something new.

Adilifu Nama added Black Panther and blaxploitation cinema into the Afrofuturist mix. While blaxploitation traded in "fantastic representations of urban blackness" that essentially turned its heroes to superheroes, he argues that "it would take black superheroes in the comic book idiom to fully transform African Americans into futuristic figures reimagined beyond the confines of enslavement, Jim Crow segregation, social sub-servience, and the inner-city blues of the black ghetto."[11]

Superhero adventures were already a kind of science fiction, after all, and the superhero already utopian. From the get-go, Superman was both a Man of Steel, adequate to the stresses and traumas of industrial culture, and a Man of Tomorrow, embodying forward-thinking American modernity. Through two world wars, machineries of destruction operated over ever greater distances and possessed increasing powers to obliterate, but on the covers of his comic books, Superman smashed ships, tanks, and planes (though he never won the war). A culture steeped in technological trauma had produced its own superhuman antidote, its own reparative fantasy. The resurgence in superhero popularity in the Silver Age had a lot to do with the powers harnessed or unleashed in the atomic age, the jet age, and the space age: human-technology relations were again front and center, as were heroism and modernity. Costumes became sleek and newly streamlined. Hal Jordan (Green Lantern) was a test pilot like the Mercury astronauts, a hero even *before* aliens gave him a power ring.[12]

Nama views *Black Panther* as more science fiction than superhero movie, going so far as to claim it as "the definitive black science fiction film and in many ways the first."[13] This brings us to the borders of Wakanda, the primary site of *Black Panther*'s science fictional imagination.

Wakanda sets Black Panther apart from all his Black super-hero brethren.[14] How does it happen that the first mainstream Black superhero is African rather than African American? An African character could operate more freely as a fantasy figure rather than as a superpowered commentary on American race relations. Wakanda represented a break from the unresolved legacies of slavery as well as the mean streets and political fractiousness of America in the 1960s. For Samantha Pinto, "the geographic distance from Africa as an actual place seems to license this fantasy of freedom to exist for African Americans in Africa itself, frozen in time."[15] "Never mind that most of us had never been to Africa," Carvell Wallace writes. "The point was not verisimilitude or a precise accounting of Africa's reality. It was the envisioning of a free self."[16]

When I think of the alternative reality that Wakanda presents, I flash back to the epiphany Richard Pryor had in the '80s while visiting Africa: "A voice said to me, 'Look around—what do you see?' and I saw all colors of people doing everything. And the voice said, 'Do you see any n*****s?' 'No.' 'Cause there *aren't* any.'"[17] African Blacks weren't second-class citizens and hadn't been dehumanized by the mechanisms of enslavement—this term of abjection had no relevance to their world.[18] Pryor immediately dropped the word from his act. In politer language, this, too, is what Wakanda offered the African American diaspora: a place of pride, untainted by the Middle Passage and its aftermath.

Again one bumps up against the untidiness of popular culture, where the creation of an African superhero and his homeland can be understood alternately as a safe retreat from reality or as a more radical imagining of another way of being in the world.

The adventures of all the streetwise Black superheroes that followed Black Panther directly engaged, by definition, the present-day struggles of Black Americans in what we used to call the urban jungle. Wakanda offered something different.

Wakanda is as much *Black Panther*'s center as the Panther himself, and he becomes a more deeply resonant character in its context. The Panther and Wakanda echo one another throughout the movie, not in a "l'état c'est moi" kind of way but rather in their shared attributes: each products of a Black utopian imagination, each traditional and futuristic, each masked and disguised and hiding in plain sight, and each negotiating a place in a larger world. They even share a musical theme. "One of the most noble aims of *Black Panther*," writes Steven Thrasher in *Esquire*, "is how it dreams of and conceives of an intact Black body—both the intact national body of Wakanda as well as the actual intact body of T'Challa in his suit."[19] Both nation and body present an idealized topos.

The nation was introduced right along with the character, back in the pages of *Fantastic Four*. The super-team is headed to Africa to meet that mystery-chieftain. Meanwhile (as they say in the comics), the reader is taken to Wakanda, a seemingly typical African village, which is to say we get warriors with spears and shields, native pots, animal skins, robed figures, and trays of what might be tropical fruits. But at the command "Raise the totem! Let the ritual begin!," a "strange carved figure" rises from a "hidden underground silo." The king exposes a "bank of electronic computers," deftly checks the status of his "devices," and removes his "stalking costume from its carefully concealed compartment." We next see the garbed Black Panther in the original version of his sleek "stalking costume."[20]

By now the Fantastic Four have arrived in Wakanda to discover, beneath the dense foliage, a "man-made jungle." The comic erupts into an oversize panel crawling with sinuous Jack Kirby technologies. "The entire topography and flora are electronically-controlled **mechanical apparatus**! The very

**branches** about us are composed of delicately-constructed **wires**... while the **flowers** which abound here are highly complex buttons and dials!" And, my favorite sentence *ever*: "Even the **boulders** can be heard to hum with the steady pulse of **computer dynamos**!"[21]

*High-tech Wakanda.* Black Panther, *vol. 1, no. 52 (July 1966). Jack Kirby (pencils), Joe Sinnott (inks).*

This is Afrofuturist as all get out: it's futuristic, technologized, set in Africa, and grounded in an alternative history of an unconquered continent. Plus it's in a comic book, a sub-legitimate medium if ever there was one. It fits all the stylistic and conceptual criteria. But it was created by those two white guys, Lee and Kirby. If we follow Dery to the letter, then Wakanda isn't Afrofuturist by reason of its provenance; at the same time, though, it's too seminal to exclude. Wakanda was, at the very least, Afrofuturist avant la lettre, and it served as a template for plenty of Afrofuturist visions to come. Afrofuturist concepts and artworks are "constellated from far-flung points," and its practitioners appropriate and repurpose non-Black popular cultural artifacts all the time.[22] As Carvell Wallace put it, "Black folks wasted no time in recolonizing Wakanda."[23]

Later *Panther* comics eschewed or downplayed Wakanda's Afrofuturism. There was little high tech on display in McGregor's "Panther's Rage," and Priest was more interested in taking T'Challa to the streets than in exploring a science fictional never-never land. Wakanda was immediately central to the comics scripted by Ta-Nehisi Coates, though he was initially more invested in its politics than its techno-futurist possibilities. But then he took readers to the Intergalactic Empire of Wakanda to assert some fine Afrofuturist mojo. Let me just repeat: *the Intergalactic Empire of Wakanda.*

Apart from some computer banks and technological jungles, Wakanda itself seems to live entirely traditionally. While writing this book I began to wonder when Wakanda became more pervasively technologized, and which writer made it so. I pored through back issues to discover that . . . it kinda just *happened*. This tells us something important about the nature of serial storytelling. I've privileged individual works and authors throughout this book, but Frank Kelleter admonishes, "When we isolate individual episodes of an initially open-ended series and then analyze these selections with tools that were developed for stand-alone works, we are probably missing something important."[24] Editorial decisions shape the directions of comics, sometimes more than any individual writer or artist. Readers chime in while awaiting the next installment, which might affect the direction of the narrative. Kelleter refers to this thicket of writers, artists, editors, media iterations, and reader/viewer feedback as a network of "distributed intention."[25] In the long history of superheroes and their worlds, elements can take shape over time without anyone in particular creating them.

Lee and Kirby provided a glimpse of an electronic jungle that did . . . something . . . and T'Challa's living quarters were modern. But other Wakandans seemed to live in the timeless clichés of "primitive" huts and "tribal" garb. Later stories presented sophisticated Wakandan defense systems and T'Challa's subterranean control center—still far from the lives of most Wakandans. In *Jungle Action* #11, the villain, Karnaj, has a technologically advanced hideout, but otherwise all the fancy tech seems to exist within the walls of the royal palace.[26] But two issues later, a modern hospital appears: "The examination rooms **blend** African sculpture with modern equipment. **Tribal herbalists** work alongside **skilled surgeons** . . . but the efforts at easing the **cultural clash** have not entirely succeeded."[27] This brings Wakanda only into the twentieth century, not a high-tech futurity. But the idea of a technologically advanced Wakanda seems fully realized in the first issue penned by Christopher Priest, in which a drunken Zuri (advisor to the king) brags about Wakanda's pioneering development of magnetic pulse technology. And in one corner of a panel in a later issue, we catch a glimpse of a high-tech, modern city of skyscrapers in the corner of a frame, as well as a "techno-jungle," a labyrinth of cables that T'Challa navigates with ease.[28]

So, somehow along the way, without anyone in particular thinking too hard about it, technology went from being the special province of the king to being something diffused throughout Wakanda.

Building upon all this, Coogler, production designer Hannah Beachler (whose credits not only include Coogler's other features but *Moonlight* and Beyoncé's *Lemonade*), costume designer Ruth E. Carter (whose extensive work with African American directors encompasses *Selma* and many of Spike Lee's films), and the rest of the *Black Panther* production team created the most compelling and coherent vision to date of an Afrofuturist Wakanda. They've done so through their deep consideration of the relations of past to present to future, steeping their vision in equal measures of history and extrapolation. It helps that they had not just the will but the resources to research and draw from and across African cultures, and to partner with progressive and well-funded design firms that could imagine and bring to the screen compelling and plausible alternative technologies.

*Black Panther*'s willingness to imagine its Afrofuturist setting and society is really where, to use a tired but for once applicable phrase, the movie transcends its genre. It not only has the feel of utopia—who *wouldn't* want to hang out in Wakanda's hipster district Step Town, with its harmonious admixture of holograms and decorative lip plates, songs and youth, and sizzling meats?—but it even edges up to showing us how it could be realized, not just through stagings of political debate but through nonrepresentational signs of color, music, and movement.

*Step Town blipsters.*

And then there are the signs, representational and not, of Wakandan design and architecture. They're representational in that they speak to Wakanda's backstory: following extensive research in Africa—including Lesotho, Senegal, South Africa, and Kenya—production designer Beachler prepared a more than five-hundred-page "bible" that did more than envision the Wakandan *now*; it sought to understand how they *got* to now. How is vibranium mined? What would advanced technological interfaces look like in a society willfully isolated from the West? What kind of urbanism might result if vibranium, rather than fossil fuels, guided architectural and planning choices? What would a society look like if the very highest technologies coexisted, without friction, with vital traditions?

These are representational signs in that they signify, at every turn, the history of Wakanda's development, but they also take on something of a nonrepresentational ambience that emerges from the way Coogler treats them. Coogler wanted audiences to feel that when the movie was over they could actually visit Wakanda. "People need to eat!" Coogler insisted; Wakanda had to be a place where people lived.[29] (Let's take it as a mark of the *Panther* team's success that a college student could give an eleven-minute presentation on the history and politics of Wakanda without the teacher realizing it wasn't a real nation.)[30]

Wakanda's central city of Birnin Zana looks a bit haphazard, its sprawl not overly planned. Like *Blade Runner*'s Los Angeles, it seems to have emerged over time. But where the future Los Angeles was retrofitted atop the industrial bones of the twentieth-century city, Birnin Zana is built upon and around traditional structures and natural landscapes. Skyscrapers sport the rounded, sometimes thatched, roofs characteristic of rondavel huts; green space flourishes between buildings and upon roofs; vines hang from balconies. There are no private cars: maglev trains and hover-buses are used for transport. In a *Forbes* article subtitled "Five Transportation Insights from *Black Panther*," one insight is that "a pedestrian-first approach cultivates culture."[31] And so the streets are unpaved dirt, comfortable for strolling. The city boasts a healthy hybridity of tradition and innovation (a theme that runs through the film, as Coogler notes in his commentary).

Shuri's ultra-high-tech lab—officially known as the Wakandan Design Group—is located within Mount Bashenga, where vibranium is mined. The entrance to the mines is adorned with a massive statue of Bast, the Panther Goddess. A circular ramp through the center of the lab links its various levels. Beachler imagined that the lab had been built around "a giant drill bit . . . created a long time ago" when vibranium mining was more industrial (primitive, by Wakandan standards). Shuri has repurposed this rocky, industrial space, making it her own with algorithmically generated kinetic art and Afrofuturist graffiti (by Brandon Sandler). (It's also very influenced by Ken Adams, the production designer for the early James Bond movies—appropriate, given that Shuri is *Black Panther*'s "Q").

Beachler drew upon the organic curvatures and intimate interiors associated with the late architect Zaha Hadid, which she combined with African regional styles and tribal decoration to create her luscious Pan-African metropolis.[32] Nature, history, and modernity entwine harmoniously. A Pan-African hybridity also manifests in the costume designs, like those for the five tribes of Wakanda, each combining patterns, fabrics, and styles from multiple regions and local traditions: the River Tribe's look, for one, is based on that of the Tsamai and Suri Tribes in southwestern Ethiopia and the Wagenia fishermen in the Democratic Republic of Congo. Futuristic elements may be literally woven in: the cloaks of the Border tribespeople (who constitute the first line of Wakandan defense) are threaded through with vibranium so they can double as shields.

By imagining different districts within the city, and by envisioning and inhabiting it so thoroughly (following the lead of such films as *Blade Runner*), the film evinces a strong sense of place. But Coogler and director of photography Rachel Morrison (who also shot Coogler's first feature, *Fruitvale Station*) choose not to linger on their marvelous setting: few encompassing views of Wakanda sprawl before our appreciative and sublimely slack-jawed faces, and there are few long takes to encourage us to linger and take it all in.

The exception, of course, is our first view of Wakanda, as T'Challa, Nakia, and Okoye approach in their Talon Fighter. "We are home," the often unsmiling Okoye says with a smile, as we see a landscape titled for us, in another language, in a special font (co-designed by Beachler and Zachary Fannin) that unscrambles to "Wakanda." Baaba Maal is heard singing in Fula, unaccompanied, on the soundtrack. Mountains and valleys, no civilization as yet. Nakia and T'Challa crowd forward. The Fighter flies low over galloping herds (notably *not* freaked out by this nearly silent flyer), waving shepherds, folks on horseback. Drums and strings are heard, with the occasional electronic swoosh of the fighter. A forested mountaintop looms; the craft doesn't slow. T'Challa (on behalf of himself, his friends, and superhero fans everywhere) murmurs, "This never gets old."[33]

The craft penetrates the veil behind which the Afrofuturist marvel of Birnin Zana, the Golden City, hides; the city materializes and spreads before the approaching craft, whose trajectory and speed the camera tracks. Talking drums swell and the music crescendos with *Black Panther*'s main orchestral theme. The camera follows, and we move with it, snaking between skyscrapers and towers (awesome in 3D). The viewer's experience is no longer filtered through anyone else's; the camera follows its own path, lowering gradually to street level. Cut to the landing area, backlit by a glorious blazing sun behind the towering towers. The Talon Fighter, which looks to be equal parts Chokwe mask and a massive set of subwoofers—when you think about it, Afrofuturism *is* a vibranium-powered Talon Fighter that looks like a Chokwe mask and a subwoofer—settles to rest where the Queen, Shuri, and troops of the Dora Milaje await.

I describe this at length for two reasons. One is that this scene is kind of my stock-in-trade when writing about science fiction film: the magisterial, panoramic, mobile gaze, only lightly mediated by the characters in the film, constitutes the best kind of cinematic attraction. It's reminiscent of

*Approaching the Golden City.*

the technological sublime evoked in special-effects sequences by Douglas Trumbull, the aerial tours in *Blade Runner* most evidently.[34] Narrative yields to the visual exploration and experience of a technologically sublime environment. Usually the characters in the narrative are blasé about the unfolding views that are, for them, quotidian. I'm charmed that Okoye, T'Challa, and Nakia react with such open pleasure to their unfolding view of their splendid home.

The other reason to linger here is that it's the *only* sequence of its kind in *Black Panther*. After this initial burst of wonder, Coogler treats Wakanda as he did Oakland in *Fruitvale Station* or Philadelphia in *Creed*: as a place where people live and work. "People need to eat!" As T'Challa and Nakia stroll the streets of Step Town, we can see citizens in the background (yes, eating) getting a visible kick out of finding the king in their midst. It's in this sense that the details over which Beachler labored become almost ambient; the movie rarely pauses long enough to fully "read" the stories told by the design elements, not because it's rushed but because it's the characters that occupy the literal, conceptual, and emotional foreground. It's not entirely clear whether Coogler explicitly rejected a more "spectacular" approach or just innately tends toward something more intimate.[35]

Two decades after Dery identified the problem, non-white and/or non-male science fiction and fantasy writers are more plentiful, more visible, and more lauded (Jemisin herself having won the Hugo Award, one of the field's highest honors, three years running, to say nothing of her 2020 MacArthur grant), yet popular culture remains one of the most fertile sites for Afrofuturist fantasy. Jemisin's own polemic, the one that began with the whiteness of *The Jetsons*, moved to a celebration of "the antidote that is Janelle Monáe."[36] She writes in a wondering tone that slightly echoes Dery's, "Everyone jokes that of course black history gets celebrated only during the shortest month of the year. No one seems puzzled by the fact that there is no time correspondingly devoted to examining, celebrating, or imagining the black future."[37] The "ultra technological future" encountered through Monáe's music and videos is bracingly welcome. It's difficult now, if not impossible, for me to think of Janelle Monáe and not of Shuri, and vice versa: two young Astro-Black women so comfortably inhabiting a technological future-alternative that they *own*.[38]

Afrofuturism is as much about alternative histories as about possible futures (the latter often predicated on the former), and Wakanda offers a potent image of an alternative Africa. The prologue animated the region's techno-fantastic history, leading to the moment when Wakanda cloaked itself beneath a briefly shimmering blue field, its secrets to conceal. The camera continues its outward movement to show an African continent devoid of light: "darkest" Africa, as the saying goes.

But this, we now know, is a false front—light hides within that darkness, behind that mask, that technological veil. The veil was a metaphor W. E. B. Du Bois deployed to mark the separateness of Black experience: "It dawned upon me with a certain suddenness that I was different from the others; or like, mayhap, in heart and life and longing, but shut out from their world by a vast veil."[39] *Black Panther* reverses the negative meaning and recasts the symbolism: the "vast veil" is no longer a tool of dehumanization, but instead is employed willfully as the secret marker of Wakanda's immunity from definitions imposed from without. Wakanda has decided how it will be seen or unseen, just as Black Panther has decided for his Black embodied self. Coates appreciates how Wakanda allegorizes the perennial question among Black Americans: "How much of ourselves can we reveal to the world?"[40] Again and again, *Black Panther* appropriates and reverses racist or racialized tropes: animality, Blackness, the veil.

Wakanda was first introduced through the lens of myth, then through the rapture of homecoming. Our next encounter is through an institution: the "Museum of Great Britain."

We first meet the adult Erik Stevens at the museum, where he's inspecting African artifacts—masks, shields, tools. We see him from the back, the camera slowly tracking toward him.[41] His hair is up and braided, he sports a couple of beaded necklaces, his fleece-collared jean jacket is well worn, and a pair of gold-rimmed glasses gives him the air of an eager grad student (and Tupac fan).[42] He's being shadowed so closely by museum security that they almost look like his posse. A curator approaches. "They tell me you're the expert," Erik says. "Ah," she answers, "you could"—modest chuckle—"say that." He asks her about various objects—age, region, provenance. After a few interchanges, his tone changes subtly: "Now ... tell me about *this* one." "Also from Benin. Seventh century. Fula Tribe, I believe." (I admire her brief admission of imperfection). "Nah," Erik replies. "It was *taken* by British soldiers in Benin, but it's *from* Wakanda. And it's made out of vibranium." He then confusingly adds, in response to her bemusement/astonishment/irritation, "Don't trip. I'm gonna take it off your hands for you." She, now entirely mystified, points out that it's not for sale, and Erik turns to her. "How do you think your ancestors got these?" His bookish mien gains an edge. "Think they paid a fair price? Or did they *take* it like they took everything *else*?"

*History lesson.*

All this is prelude to the theft of this vibranium-headed tool and the murder of the museum personnel in partnership with Ulysses Klaue, but the heist has taken on the air of a repatriation. Erik's "evil" is historicized from the moment we meet him. African nations are introduced as colonized and denuded of their cultural heritage; the museum is introduced as complicit in the plunder—with Erik as a righteously angry student of postcolonial politics. The Wakandan artifact, its vibranium head covered with a veneer of dust and rust, has made its way there by accident; the nation has been functionally invisible to the colonialist, appropriative gaze (and reach) of the Western museum. The entire scene is bathed in a light-blue tint, blue a color associated with British colonialism and the indigo trade.[43]

But we've actually met Erik twice already, though without knowing it: his was the voice in the prologue, asking questions about home and hiding, and he was one of the children who watched the mysterious Wakandan aircraft depart in the aftermath of his father's killing (a killing of which he was as yet unaware). Wakanda is introduced in terms of the colonial history of Africa, but Erik bears his own history, traumatically connected to Wakanda's. He's half Wakandan: his father was N'Jobu, on a spying mission to the United States, and Erik, his son, was simply abandoned by the Wakandans. His Wakandan name is N'Jadaka, and, as he says later, he "found [his] daddy with Panther claws in his chest."

What is the place of Wakanda in the contemporary world? What is its responsibility to *global* history? Some of its citizens and leaders want Wakanda to join the global struggle to end the abuse and poverty of Black and brown peoples: N'Jobu and his son N'Jadaka, but also W'Kabi of the Border Tribe, policing the nation's borders, and Nakia, the War Dog, who says, "I can't be happy here knowing that there's people out there who have nothing." The old guard, which includes elder tribespeople and T'Challa in his role of king, believe that Wakanda's responsibility is to itself, especially in times of upheaval ("As Wakanda thrived," N'Jobu's opening narration told us, "the world around it descended further into chaos."). When Erik, now known as Killmonger, arrives in the Tribal Council

Room, he excoriates Wakanda's rulers and elders: "Y'all sittin'
up here comfortable. Must feel good. There's about two billion
people all over the world that looks like us but their lives are
a lot harder."[44]

Wakanda has often been presented as an exceptional nation, never colonized, its peoples never enslaved: "the dream,"
writes Samantha Pinto, "of Blackness untouched and un-
scathed by white violence."[45] Its monarchical rule has been
benign, its people sharing the technological benefits of the
country's unique cache of vibranium. Various comics writers
have put Wakanda on the right side of history, whether around
apartheid or the Rwandan genocide. All too often, though,
comic book politics sets up false equivalences in order to keep
Wakanda—and Marvel—carefully neutral.

For the most part, Wakanda remains separate from actual
African history. The main existential threats have come, and
keep on coming, from folks like Namor (the Sub-Mariner), Dr.
Doom, Thanos, and the Skrulls, but (to paraphrase Stephen
Sondheim) *they're still here*. America knows there's *some*thing
of value to be had there, and Wakandan politics often involves
deflecting the American sense of entitled interest. Frankly, a
coherent history of the place couldn't be written—at times the
world seems to know of Wakanda and its power; other times it
doesn't. When T'Challa marries Storm of the X-Men (a match
inevitably compared to, and probably inspired by, the coupling
of Beyoncé and Jay-Z), they tour the world, speaking to its
leaders—hardly a low-profile event.

Wakanda is also something of a feminist utopia.

It might be asked just how progressive, or truly feminist,
a Disney/Marvel blockbuster can be; after all, we've already

covered the excruciatingly gradual centering of heretofore marginalized peoples in the superhero movie. *Black Panther* was written by two men (Ryan Coogler and Joe Robert Cole) and directed by one of them (Coogler). The central conflict in the movie is staged between two male characters (T'Challa and N'Jadaka). Wakanda's system of governance is patrilineal (Coates has tried to restructure this in the comics), and an unabashedly masculinist ritual combat—staged twice, both times between men—offers a viable path to the throne.[46] These are valid concerns, but there's more going on.

There is a shot, near one of the many endings of *Avengers: Endgame*, that I think annoyed just about everybody. Seemingly every hero, sidekick, and pet in the Marvel Cinematic Universe has been facing off against Thanos and his endless hordes of hordes. In a single shot, Captain Marvel is joined by many of the women of the MCU: the Scarlet Witch, Valkyrie, Okoye, Rescue, Mantis, Shuri, the Wasp, and Gamora (I *think* that's mostly it). Having "assembled" in this way, they rejoin the fight. Nothing connects these women beyond their gender, their momentary co-presence in a single frame, and their shared existence as properties of Marvel. For a studio that had at that time released only a single movie with a female lead (and that only recently), Marvel seemed awfully proud of itself.

Compare it to another moment, in *Black Panther*, as the Dora Milaje, Shuri, and Nakia stand against Killmonger and the Border Tribe, now loyal to him. Shuri uses her sand table to conjure weapons and armor for Nakia; they hurry from the lab, leaving a slightly hapless Agent Ross to fight a virtual drone battle in the skies. Atop Mount Bashenga, General Okoye and her troops are in fevered battle. In one tight shot, we see the weaponed hands of Shuri and Nakia enter the frame one after the other: a vibranium gauntlet, then another; a ring blade, then another. The door opens, and Shuri and Nakia defiantly come out blasting. Neither woman is a warrior—they are, respectively, a scientist and a spy—but they are proud and powerful Wakandan women, loyal to T'Challa, to their nation, and to each other.[47]

It would have been so easy for the first franchise Black superhero movie to be a testosterone-fueled slugfest. Easy to follow in the footsteps of *Shaft* and take T'Challa to the mean streets of an American city (turnabout is fair play after all; Shaft went to Africa). Easy to build up to a spectacular CGI-candy finale with lots of property damage (that got put off until *Endgame*). Other movies of the MCU manage to allocate one woman per male superhero to serve as reassurer, pragmatist, assistant, and/or cuddler. Easy for Marvel to import Black Panther's sometime girlfriend from the comics, Monica Lynne, a soul singer and a good listener.

With the hunger for a Black superhero as strong as it was, that film might yet have done well; it might have broken records, made history. But its cultural relevance would have been diminished. We would never have experienced Wakanda's Afrofuturist and Pan-African glories, and—most depressingly—we would have missed the power of its feminism, which goes by the names Nakia, Okoye, Shuri, and Ramonda. *Black Panther* is filled with strong, accomplished women, only one of whom might be dating T'Challa (and that isn't even *her* primary role). The feminism of *Black Panther* isn't highlighted in the film's title, but like Wakanda itself, it's hiding in plain sight and has been noted by fans, scholars, and critics alike.

Coates led the way in the comics, giving the Milaje an

expanded role and focusing on a queer Milaje couple in his first story arc.

The Panther's most trusted counselors are women. Nakia is one of Wakanda's War Dogs; she works undercover beyond Wakanda's borders. Shuri, T'Challa's teen sister, is very explicitly the movie's Q (tech maker to James Bond), but she's also a fighter, a surgeon, and an inspiration to STEM programs everywhere.[48] Okoye leads the Dora Milaje, the king's female cohort of bodyguards and warriors. These are far from the wives-in-waiting introduced in the comics, and they no longer look like clubgoers as they did in the Christopher Priest–scripted comics.[49] The Queen Mother, Ramonda, is T'Challa's mother and T'Chaka's widow; following her son's "death" she spearheads the attempt to remove Killmonger from the throne.[50]

Diana Adesola Mafe's work on Black female characters in moving image speculative fiction provides a helpful way to think about women and performance in *Black Panther*. While science fiction "has certainly been complicit in sustaining and even promoting social prejudices against Others . . . it has also been a remarkable site of possibility when it comes to interrogating and reinventing social constructs such as race, gender, and class."[51] The superhero genre, too—in part an offshoot of science fiction—has begun to move beyond its masculinist and often misogynistic roots (not that those don't still exist in abundance).

Mafe's character case studies exhibit striking levels of agency, resist marginalization, exceed the containments of the male gaze, turn stereotypes on their heads, are self-defining, and act heroically in ways that often involve saving the non-Black, non-female heroes they accompany. In language

*Women of Wakanda.*

reminiscent of hooks and Smith and Cobb (see the preceding chapter), she claims her chosen characters as "important countermodels."[52] All of this works for the women of Wakanda.

The women are largely in charge, and the casting is as strong as the characters: Angela Bassett (Ramonda), Lupita Nyong'o (Nakia), actor and sometime playwright Danai Gurira (Okoye), and Letitia Wright (Shuri).[53] Performance is the least considered aspect of filmmaking—an especially unfortunate oversight, when it's arguably the element least under a director's control—yet it can introduce resonances that might amplify or destabilize the "meaning" of a movie or scene. Andrew Klevan's study of Barbara Stanwyck argues that *Stella Dallas* and *Double Indemnity*, the Stanwyck movies that have generated the most contradictory interpretations, become more coherent when her layered performances are considered; her versions of the self-sacrificing mother and the femme fatale undermine those very archetypes.[54] Performers, too, have agency, make choices.[55]

The actors playing the women of Wakanda are less ancillary to the male hero than Mafe's examples are. They don't need to serve a subversive function since the movie builds strong, challenging roles around them, but they enhance its feminism by imbuing their characters with presence, intensity, and, not least, humor. On the Nigerian mission, Black Panther and Okoye have liberated the kidnapped women and one of the child-militants, and are about to send them home. Okoye commands them with a hiss: "You will speak *nothing* of this day." The *barest* hint of a smile softens her steely gaze, a humanizing moment visibly appreciated by these traumatized captives. The script reads: "T'Challa looks at the Young Militant for a

beat before he, Nakia and Okoye disappear through the trees."
What's missing here is the smile with which Okoye lets them
(and us) briefly see that she's something more than yet another
archetype: in this case, the phallic woman warrior.[56]

It's not necessary to claim that Gurira improvised this, or
snuck it in while nobody was looking, or was following direction, to associate *this* particular expression, *this* gesture by
*this* character, with the compelling body of the performer on
screen. And when those bodies are Black women, four Black
women actors, four Black women actors who are playing four
Black women very different from one another . . . something
significant is happening in this corporate blockbuster. "Given
the often-stereotypical depictions and thin roles often available
for Black women actors," observes Robyn Spencer, "any two
of these characters in a film would be notable. The presence
of all of them was nothing short of path breaking."[57] To which
I'd add, the presence of all of them in a *superhero movie* . . . I
mean, come *on*.

*Black Panther* is richly acted throughout, and the movie
belongs as much to the supporting cast as to Boseman and
Jordan. They're not even the only movie stars: you've got
Nyong'o and Bassett and Daniel Kaluuya (W'Kabi). It's as close
to an all-star movie as the genre has fielded and as much an
ensemble work as any Avengers outing. Back in 2016, Wesley
Morris legitimately worried that "the comic-book franchise
is where traditional movie stardom is going to die" (the
superhero-as-star trumping the actor-as-star), but, at least in
the case of *Black Panther* and a few other movies from the past
few years, things are looking up.[58]

Nakia and Okoye have political roles to play: Okoye is tormented but staunch in her loyalty to the throne, whomsoever

sits upon it. Upon T'Challa's return, she leads the Dora Mi- laje in the wrenching battle against Killmonger's Border Tribe supporters, who are led by her husband, W'Kabi.[59] She is not swayed by sentimentality, but is sensibly relieved when she no longer needs to do her sworn duty to, you know, kill him.

Shuri and Nakia are conduits to the outside world. Shuri is sassy in a little sister way, hip to internet memes ("WHAT ARE THOSE!"[60]) and rude gestures, and proud of her accomplishments—note her appreciation of Agent Ross's ap- preciation of what she and Wakanda have built. The affec- tion between sister and brother is charming; when T'Challa saunters into her lab with his retinue she solemnly bows: "My king." They giggle and perform an elaborate and very contem- porary handshake, as ritualized as anything in the movie. But while Shuri may be on the grid, she's not blindly seduced by the West: surprised by Ross, she jumps and exclaims, "Don't scare me like that, colonizer!" Jelani Cobb reports that the audience he saw the film with "howled at the inversion, 'col- onizer' deployed as an epithet rather than a badge of cultural superiority."[61]

Nakia is the first to confront T'Challa with an alternative politics for Wakanda, which sounds not unlike N'Jobu's plan from the Oakland prologue. The movie seems to stage a di- chotomy between isolationist T'Challa and interventionist Killmonger, hero versus villain, but the ideological chasm be- tween them is actually occupied by others—Nakia first among them—who envision another way (to be discussed further in the next chapter). Jonathan Gray aligns her with the "new gen- eration of female activists rising in Africa, like the Nobel Peace Laureate Leymah Gbowee, who has promoted the cultivation of soft power to diffuse war."[62] Nakia doesn't even want to live in Wakanda, however utopic it might be, if it remains above the fray. She may be the movie's love interest—to the extent that it has one—but she is never reduced to, or limited by, that role.

But *Black Panther* isn't all politics, and T'Challa needs these women for more than their polemical positions. Early in the movie, when T'Challa goes to retrieve Nakia from her mission, he tells Okoye that he doesn't need her help. She gives a brief and telling "hm" and instructs him not to freeze. T'Challa smiles, oozing Boseman confidence: "What are you talking about?"—his tone is musical, amused—"I never freeze." When he sees Nakia, though, he will, yes, freeze: in the midst of the mayhem he sees her, stops in his tracks, and squeezes out a most un-superhero-y ". . . Hi." Okoye abruptly appears to save them all, having wisely ignored his command. Nakia, Okoye, and Black Panther fight together: not a super-team like the Avengers or the Suicide Squad, but no less a team.

Upon their arrival in Wakanda, Shuri asks Okoye, "Did he freeze?" "Like an antelope in headlights." The two speak a shared language while they share a laugh at the expense of our male hero, our superhero king.

So, the car chase I promised to discuss way back in the preface: more Marvel movies feature car chases than I thought, and *Black Panther*'s is pretty good. Like the fight in Nigeria, this, too, involves Okoye and Nakia (in one car) and adds teenage Shuri to the mix, giddily driving a remote car from back in Wakanda, out of harm's way. Klaue and his henchmen have come to a very James Bond secret casino in Busan to sell some vibranium to the American agent Ross, who's quite surprised to find a bunch of Wakandans crashing his party.

Things go south, a well-choreographed fight ensues

(using the long takes Coogler employed in his boxing movie, *Creed*), and Klaue and company escape in a small fleet of Toyota 4Runners. Okoye drops a kimoyo bead onto a Lexus LC, which allows Shuri to access its controls. Black Panther does an elegant little backflip onto the hood, and the chase is on.[63] "Woo! Let's go," Shuri yells. A bit later, she'll run over a dropped body: "What was that?" she wonders from Wakanda. "Don't worry about it!" her brother answers. "You're doing great!" Nakia drives a Lexus GS-F with Okoye riding shotgun. The bad guys begin spraying them with machine gun fire, to which they react with calm disdain: "Guns. [Pause] So primitive." They're reclining easily in their seats; though Nakia steers with determination, the muted sound in their car makes it all somehow soothing. Okoye climbs out the car window to the roof, red dress billowing behind her, wielding her spear like a mad harpoonist; she skewers one of the 4Runners from rear bumper to front end, pinioning it in place.

The Panther has some good moves, too, but we're not talking about him now.

The car driven by Nakia and Okoye gets destroyed, as happens in these things: Klaue's sonic cannon practically disintegrates it around them. They come to an anti-climactically slow stop, Okoye skidding but upright on a piece of car roof, Nakia behind a wheel no longer connected to a car.[64]

This is different from what Iris Young described as the learned condition of "inhibited intentionality" that circumscribes how too many women occupy space and their own bodies. Throwing like a girl is learned behavior. But just as Black superheroes offer a recuperative fantasy of visibility and enhanced powers to act upon the world, recent female action heroes offer alternative phenomenologies. The genius of *Birds of Prey (and the Fantabulous Emancipation of One Harley Quinn)* is the unfettered, free movement of one Harley Quinn, as she takes out a flock of bad guys with nothing more than her favored weapon, a baseball bat—emphatically *not* "swinging like a girl."[65] The genius of *Black Panther* is Okoye "made" by the bad guys at the casino, flinging her hated wig-disguise into the face of a thug, extending her spear, and kicking off the action sequence; or non-warriors Shuri and Nakia, lined up and coordinated, ready to defend their nation when that door opens. Changing the rules, choosing their roles: that none of them are superheroes seems not to inhibit them at all.

The point is that the women of Wakanda are full participants in the political process and the action scenes, in serious matters as well as the more kinetic and comic entertainments. The car chase is great good fun, and Okoye, Shuri, and even Nakia (who's usually pretty serious) provide their fair share of it. Black Panther never fights alone until the final battle with Killmonger, deep in the vibranium mine—while Shuri, Okoye, and Nakia are combatants in the civil war taking place above.

For all of that, though, it's still true that men sit atop the hierarchy of Wakandan power. Ramonda's first choice to replace T'Challa as Black Panther is Nakia, whose refusal feels kind of pro forma: "I'm a spy with no army. I wouldn't stand a chance." As Tolulope Akinwole puts it, "Female leadership in Wakanda is not foreclosed, even if one wonders why the movie stops short of imagining it."[66] In that context, it's disappointing to learn that Shuri—daughter, after all, of King T'Chaka—might not become the next Black Panther in place of the now-absent T'Challa. She took on the role in the comics scripted by Reginald Hudlin but won't on the big screen (as far as I know at the time I'm writing).[67] Yes, I'm sure there are legitimate concerns about Letitia Wright's ability to open a $300 million movie, but it would be awfully fun.[68]

Nevertheless, Black Panther—more than any superhero in a movie that isn't about a team—doesn't work alone. To the extent that T'Challa escapes the objectification Charles Johnson refers to as "the black as body situation," it has much to do with the support he has from the nation of Wakanda generally, but from these women in particular. Black Panther is more than just a heart-shaped herb and an inherited title. He is also a part of something larger: a family, a community, Wakanda.[69]

Wakanda is Afrofuturist, it presents an alternative history of Africa, and its women are central to its functioning. It also speaks to a utopic, Pan-African present.

And Wakanda's present is drenched in *color*. The superhero genre is (or should be) a colorful one, but *Black Panther*'s chromatic richness derives from more than its costumed hero.[70] Color, in more than one sense, is celebrated throughout the movie, but especially in the lengthy sequence that extends from the celebration of the gathering of the tribes for T'Challa's challenge ceremony to the new king's spiritual pilgrimage to the Hall of Kings and visit to the Ancestral Plane (a space out of time, both real and mythic).

Wakandan tradition and high technology combine in the challenge ceremony, perhaps the movie's finest set piece. The scene presents a mélange of aesthetics, dances, and musics. Barges carrying representatives of Wakanda's stylistically distinct tribes approach Warrior Falls. The warriors of the Dora Milaje, in ceremonial uniforms, perform a jumping dance to the intricate beat of the drums that echo from the barges. The tribes are resplendent in their colors: shades of green for the

River Tribe, blues for the Border Tribe, reds for the Miners, purple for the Merchants. Everyone is costumed and bedecked with beadwork and embroidery; elaborate necklaces of bells and beads of many shapes and colors, some with metallic embellishments; massive golden earrings; complicated plaits; and face paint.

Shuri and Nakia, the two characters most connected to and invested in the world beyond Wakanda, participate with evident pleasure. Shuri dances with the Queen Mother, her face and hair framed with beads and bones. On another barge, Nakia dances while everyone sways, claps, and sings in joyous support; she's resplendent in the vivid green tones of the River Tribe, her face paint perhaps suggesting the Panther totem. A tribal elder with a face plate is bedecked in long robes; a shawl bespeaks his rank, and he sports a massive headpiece of ivory or bone. The camera moves around and through the scene as everyone approaches Warrior Falls, where the ceremony will take place.

A signal from the Dora Milaje opens massive drains that lower the water around the falls in preparation for the challenge; the Royal Talon Fighter bearing the heir to the throne settles into place. Stepping from the craft, T'Challa is greeted by the towering sight of all the tribal representatives and celebrants arrayed from the bottom to the top of a steep rock wall; to the sound of drums, the camera pans across pockets of intense color and rapturous movement, framed by the wonders of the natural landscape. It's among the most striking shots of the movie, though briefer than I'd like it to be. I'm going to freeze-frame it for a moment to appreciate its chromatically rich presence . . .

Western culture is understood to have a long-standing

suspicion of vivid color: David Batchelor writes that in the West "colour has been systematically marginalized, reviled, diminished and degraded."[71] Non-Western cultures incorporate color more thoroughly and more boldly into clothing, adornment, ritual, and art, but color is oppositional to the "virtuous whiteness of the West," where it's regulated and tamed. Michael Taussig finds bold colors in only the occasional, carefully limited, flourish: "Safe in your whiteness, you can hang a wildly colored picture on the wall, secure in its framed being."[72] The West marginalizes the sensual corruptions of color by relegating it "to the realm of the superficial, the supplementary, the inessential or the cosmetic," or by making it "the property of some 'foreign' body—usually the feminine, the oriental, the primitive, the infantile, the vulgar, the queer or the pathological."[73] It's either trivial or dangerous.

Goethe believed that "savage nations, uneducated people, and children have a great predilection for vivid colours."[74] I would playfully note that Wakanda's dancing "savages" are all of the above: assuredly "foreign," ostensibly "primitive," and possibly "oriental" (as in, exotic)—chromatic richness encompasses the people and their costumes. The crude coloring of early comic books marked them as the property of children; no adult could be charmed by those garish hues. There's a whiff of this same chromophobia in all the superhero movies that tone down the aggressive comic book colors of the costumes in the name of "realism." Even the Hulk seems a bit less green.

The vivacious colors on display at Warrior Falls remind me of Michael Powell and Emeric Pressburger's Technicolor *Black Narcissus* (1947), in which British nuns in stark white habits establish a mission in the polychromatic world of the high Himalayas. The Indigenous peoples are introduced in a brief montage: women with rich skin tones in pink and orange headscarves and turquoise beads, a woman in a blue shawl with beaded brass earrings and a red beaded necklace, a child with a colorful braided headpiece. The self-abnegatingly pure nuns struggle against the seductive chromatic and sensory power of this heightened environment, their hard work and penance no match for the radiant silks, ethereally blue skies, and unstoppably blossoming flora. A nun sacrifices the vegetable garden in favor of voluptuous flowers. Another sister's heretofore repressed lust ends tragically.

All this could be understood as *deeply* chromophobic—pure white women contaminated by colorful "savages"—but the movie, like all of the filmmakers' work, is entirely on the side of color.[75] The anxious chromophobic conflation of color and people of color, what Taussig calls the "Western experience of colonization as colored Otherness," is replaced by celebration.[76] Batchelor points out that chromophilia and chromophobia are largely identical: "Colour remains other" for the chromophile, and, "in fact, it often becomes more other than before. More dangerous, more disruptive, more excessive."[77] But the chromophile craves what the chromophobe fears. Color in *Black Narcissus* and *Black Panther* isn't symbolic or meaningful—it's immersive, tactile, palpably *present.* (Let's acknowledge one signal difference between the movies, though: the Indigenous people featured in *Black Narcissus* are largely marginalized, while in *Black Panther* they're the main event.)[78]

The critic Dave Hickey characterized the utopian rush of Saturday morning cartoons as a "wall of vibrant moving color," and *Black Panther* presents a literal wall of chromatic and cultural vibrancy, celebrating Africa, African sounds, African adornments, and African colors.[79] After T'Challa's victory over M'Baku, the Jabari Tribe's challenger, he again faces his people. The camera pulls back to revel again in this spectacular display of the power of color and people of color, shouting in unison, "Wakanda forever!"

*Warrior Falls. A wall of many colors (trust me).*

Though color in *Black Panther* is largely "more a presence than a sign," the movie also deploys it more meaningfully.[80] Purple is associated with the spiritual. For not only does Wakanda speak in its vibranium richness to a utopic future and through its never-conquered status to an alternative history, it exists, too, on a mythic plane, signified through the saturated purples and violets of the fog-enshrouded Hall of Kings. Here T'Challa will, for the first time, visit the Ancestral Plane.[81] He reclines on a bed of rust-red sand, a toothed and beaded necklace upon his chest. Zuri and other attendants in paints and purple robes prepare him; a glowing blossom of the heart-shaped herb that gives the Panther his powers is ground to a paste that Zuri dilutes and administers, invoking the presence of T'Chaka. T'Challa's muscles glow purply beneath his dark skin (colors, Taussig writes, "illuminate the backdrop of myths and

set the body alight").[82] At a command, children, decorated
and painted, shovel the rust-red sand atop T'Challa's brown
and purple body until it covers him and the screen goes black.
T'Challa "awakens" on the Ancestral Plane, a vast savannah
(the script calls it a "vast grassland," or we could, I suppose, call
it a "plain") spreading beneath an enormous, pulsingly violet
aurora. Panther-ancestors crouch in the branches of a splendid
acacia tree, their eyes aglow in the dark light. As white-robed
T'Challa approaches them, one drops to the ground and rises
as T'Chaka, wearing humble, but golden, tribal robes. T'Challa
bows to his father, who bids him to rise. Later, the Ancestral
Plane will become a scene of confrontation, but here it is a
place of timeless peace.

*T'Challa on the Ancestral Plane.*

Just as the (Academy Award–winning) production designer
Beachler drew from both traditional and modern African ar-
chitectures in Maghreb, Northern Cameroon, and the Central
African Republic, the (Academy Award–winning) costume designer Ruth E. Carter—whose career is marked by her cham-
pioning movies directed by African Americans—amalgamated
elements of costumes and adornment from across Africa:

Lesotho, north-central Kenya, South Sudan, Ethiopia, the coast of the Democratic Republic of Congo, Mali, and the Sahara.[83] And the (Academy Award–winning) composer Ludwig Göransson toured with Baaba Maal in Senegal, recorded local musicians, and immersed himself in field recordings made throughout Africa at the International Library of African Music in Grahamstown, South Africa.

The goal was always to create a Pan-African Wakanda: a Wakanda that might occupy a specific position on a geographical map but whose aesthetic spoke to a utopian synthesis. Wakanda's population is dispersed among the five tribes, each with their own aesthetic and cultural references. In this way, the unity of Wakanda speaks to the diversity of the African continent, a classic synecdoche. "Wakanda is not a country in Africa, it *is* Africa," write Ainehi Edoro and Bhakti Shringarpure, not exactly approvingly. For the movie has spawned the term "Wakandafication"—the homogenization of African cultures into something singular and ahistorical, more palatable (*too* palatable, is the suggestion) to white audiences. A flattening, rather than an honoring, of diversity, an aesthetics divorced from regional histories and traditions. Edoro and Shringarpure, for example, were disappointed to find a Wakanda "too rooted in an Africa we already know," an aesthetic too "typically anthropological," and "a very American imagination at work."[84]

The South African historian Bill Nasson also found "something familiar about this picture. The lost African world, its mother lode, its noble hereditary heroes and their impetuous, hotheaded rivals to power, formed a staple of both Britain's cinema of colonial empire, and of Hollywood's ancient world epics. . . . Now, as then, the distant kingdom is the stuff of epic."[85] Stereotypical ideas of exoticism abound: "colorful" natives, "primitive" rituals, a land of "mystery." Edoro and Shringarpure wonder why the super-advanced Wakandans haven't "managed to generate their own unique culture."[86] (They're among the few to deride the movie for not being exotic *enough*.)

It's a question. Why *not* a full-bore Afrofuturist extravaganza, filled with the hoverbikes and other wonders of vibranium that so dazzle Agent Ross? Why the Pan-Africanism, the ... Wakandafication? In flattening Africa into a stereotypical idea of "Africa," have the filmmakers fallen prey to the same exoticist clichés they wanted to subvert? Am I too fulsome in my praise of what are, after all, the movie's "colorful natives"?[87]

The thing is, Wakandafication long predates the advent of Wakanda. For more than a century, utopian dreams of a Pan-African "identity" have been critiqued for emphasizing commonality over difference. Dreams of Pan-African unity emerged from the diaspora, an appropriation of the "idea of Africa" imposed upon a diverse continent by white cultures. African Americans in the late nineteenth century—ripped from their homes across Africa and thrown together in the "new world"—began to consider Africa as a unified entity, bound by the commonality of race: a *motherland* (which was the working title for *Black Panther*—an early clue as to the centrality of Wakanda to the project).[88]

Valerie Babb situates Wakanda within a long history of Black speculative fiction, particularly in work from the late nineteenth to the early twentieth century. Citing the extensive research by *Black Panther*'s makers, she sees the movie "in dialogue with black traditions that have long engaged with ideas of a utopian Africa, the legacies of enslavement, and black power, both human and technological."[89] Alternate histories, hidden lands, technological prowess, and "super" heroes abound in these works, in which "black speculative writers look[ed] to the past and pair[ed] imagined African origins with Afrofuturist content to compensate for a historical record that does not recognize black achievement."[90]

The Pan-African dream itself has always been unabashedly utopian, an attempt to intertwine Indigenous and diasporic populations to heal the sundering of Africa's peoples through enslavement and colonization. Pan-African proponents and speculative fiction writers, then, share a utopian mindset, more wishful than naive.

*Black Narcissus* was not made on location but at Pinewood Studios in Buckinghamshire, with some exterior shooting in the far reaches of West Sussex. Its sensuous world is imaginary—a function of miniatures, glass paintings, film stocks, and performance. *Brigadoon*, too, was studio-bound, on stage and on screen. *Black Panther* was primarily shot in studios (and locations) in and around Atlanta, with some African location work. Warrior Falls itself is a green-screened composite of studio work and footage of the Iguazu Falls of South America. *Black Panther*'s "Africa" is as gloriously synthetic as the "Scottish Highlands" of *Brigadoon* or the "Himalayas" of *Black Narcissus*. All these places hold truths, even as they are patently not "real."

The *New Yorker* writer and scholar Jelani Cobb admires *Black Panther*'s imaginative appropriation of the idea of Africa, "a continent that has been grappling with invented versions of itself ever since white men first declared it the 'dark continent' and set about plundering its people and resources." Remember his claim that Wakanda "is no more or less imaginary than the Africa conjured by Hume or Trevor-Roper, or the one canonized in such Hollywood offerings as 'Tarzan.'"[91] As a locus for a *Black* idea of Africa, this product of a "very American imagination" offers what Cobb calls "a redemptive counter-mythology."[92] For Babb, Wakanda "embodies what Africa as an invention has meant in much of the black American imagination: a utopian memory, a site for creating traditions and narratives filling the lacunae of slavery, a means of establishing continuity between the black African past and the black American present."[93] What utopia would feel like.[94]

Coates has pointed out that *Black Panther* is a Pan-African movie not just in what it espouses but in its very being: "At various times onscreen you'll have a Black person from South Africa, a Black person from Kenya by way of Mexico, a Black person from London, a Black person from Trinidad and Tobago." He notes the Blackness of the movie's crew.

Rather than a documentary (or "anthropological") approach that would make of Wakanda a real place, Cobb recognizes in the movie a heightened rhetoric "shot through with the sense of longing and romance common to the way that people of a diaspora envision their distant homeland."[95] In Carvell Wallace's thoughtful interview with Coogler, both express that same sensibility. Wallace asks whether African Americans could ever fully be part of what was left behind. Coogler "dipped his head, fell briefly quiet and then looked back at me with a solemn expression. 'I think we can,' he said. 'It's no question. It's almost as if we've been brainwashed into thinking that we can't have that connection.'"[96] Ananya Jahanara Kabir writes that "the fictive nature of both this script and the Africa it signifies is neither disguised nor apologized for; Wakanda is the shape that dreams of futures past must take."[97]

But, as in the mythic Scottish village of Brigadoon, there is trouble in this "African Eden," and *Black Panther* will move beyond celebration to express what Kabir calls "an underlying longing and sorrow at deracination that is the burden of the African American as diasporic subject," a longing and sorrow (and rage) embodied by one Erik Killmonger.[98]

# The Killmonger Problem

A flurry of articles appearing shortly after *Black Panther*'s release proffered profoundly different, even opposed, readings of its politics, all of which centered on the "villain," Erik Killmonger. To understand the movie's politics, it seems, one must understand Killmonger, and one can't understand Killmonger, it seems, without seeing him through the lens of his politics. The pervading question is: Should Killmonger be regarded as representative, and if he is (or if he isn't), what is he representative (or not representative) *of*? *Black Panther* seemed to court the controversy. To return to James Wilt's assessment, the first Black blockbuster didn't *have* to be set in Africa, it didn't *have* to stage an ideological debate around racial injustice and responsibility, and it didn't *have* to leave out other, whiter, and more time-tested Avengers. "But it did."[1]

The plot of *Black Panther* is structured around a political conflict of incalculably greater consequence than whether or not superheroes should be regulated by the state.[2] The terms of the conflict resonate to Wakanda's borders and beyond—it's *about* borders. Within the history of a larger world in which Black peoples have been so constantly oppressed for so long, Killmonger asks, entirely reasonably, "Where was Wakanda?" What *is* Wakanda's proper responsibility? What do the haves owe the have-nots? If you're Black, who are your "people"?

T'Challa's friend W'Kabi of the Border Tribe is an isolationist who favors the strong borders that have long protected never-conquered, never-colonized Wakanda. The Trumpian echo to his words doesn't inspire trust: "You let refugees in, they bring their problems with them." (My favorite Marvel movie dig at Trump, though, is in *Captain Marvel*, when an alien refers to Earth as "a real shithole.") Nakia argues for change: "Share what we have. We could provide aid and access to technology and refuge to those who need it." T'Challa objects: "If the world found out what we truly are, and what we possess, we could lose our way of life." Nakia's reply: "Wakanda is strong enough to help others and protect ourselves at the same time." Killmonger wants to put Wakanda and the might of its vibranium weaponry at the center of the global struggle for Black liberation.

Nakia's perspective will win out, after T'Challa has confronted his father's lies around the murder of N'Jobu and consequent orphaning of his son, and after Killmonger's seething, uncontainable hatred has been purged from the community. Wakanda will take steps to engage the world, beginning with the establishment of the first Wakandan International Outreach Center on the very spot in Oakland where N'Jobu died and "Killmonger" was born.

Some saw *Black Panther* as espousing a liberal democratic sensibility, with Killmonger a somewhat sympathetic character whose resonant call for justice is undermined—but not negated—by the violent intervention he advocates.[3] Others, including Wilt, regarded the movie as "liberaliz[ing] black resistance for white comfort"; here, Erik's violence, far from aberrant, is a fundament of an overtly radical Black liberation politics. He plunges Wakanda into civil war, but his death marks the end of the movement's extremism, replacing more urgent and aggressive intervention with Wakanda's meek "sharing" of its technology through some lame outreach centers. Leslie Lee III articulated this position in an incendiary, and oft-retweeted, tweet: "*Black Panther* is a deeply evil film. It dangles the idea of global black liberation in front of you, paints that as villainous, then ends in an orgy of the freest black people to ever walk the earth slaughtering each other to protect whites. That shit turned my stomach."[4]

Slavoj Žižek, on the other hand, and without much effort, positioned Killmonger as *Black Panther*'s true hero.[5]

The conflict between T'Challa and Killmonger was sometimes cast as a kind of Martin Luther King Jr.–Malcolm X struggle, but *Black Panther* just isn't that reductive, not about Panther and Killmonger *or* about MLK and Malcolm X.[6] King was more than "dreams" and nonviolence and, near the end of his life, addressed the more intractable, and less "friendly," issue of wealth inequality, while Malcolm X found value in King's methods. That's not to say there's none of this in the movie: Michael B. Jordan has said he "prayed hard and meditated on people like Malcolm X and Tupac Shakur," and Malcolm X also inspired the treatment of the mutant villain Magneto in the X-Men movies (with Professor X as *his* MLK).[7] But there's more (and less) to the conflict than that. Rachel Gillett and Valerie Babb both locate the Panther and Killmonger within a longer history of ideological argument: the "clash of views" of Gaston Monnerville and Stépane Ross around French colonialism, Leopold Senghor and Frantz Fanon in the context of Négritude and Pan-Africanism, Du Bois and Marcus Garvey on the literal place of and for Black Americans—all centered on what Babb refers to as "contrasting strategies of social uplift . . . one advocating immediate, and if necessary violent, action . . . and the other advocating a more nuanced response." She points out, though, that these "seeming binaries" are "frequently exaggerated by popular discourse to mark clear parameters within debates over black political progress."[8]

Were Erik simply a Malcolm manqué, then his defeat might indeed read as a repudiation of both his means and goals. But Erik is fired by something more personal than ideological. CIA agent Ross recognizes him as "one of ours": he served with the SEALs in Afghanistan, "where he racked up confirmed kills like it was a video game" (hence "Killmonger") and belonged to a Joint Special Operations Command ghost unit, whose agents "drop off the grid so they can commit assassinations and take down governments." In this read, Erik is no Malcolm—he has no "mission" beyond destabilization. His discussions of colonial appropriation and the rights of the "two billion people all over the world" are, then, more opportunistic than political.

Adam Serwer of the *Atlantic* saw Killmonger's advocacy of Black liberation as a blind for his real goal of world domination: a dream of empire, with Wakanda its center and Killmonger its emperor.[9] "*Black Panther* does not render a verdict that violence is an unacceptable tool of black liberation—to the contrary, that is precisely how Wakanda is liberated. It renders a verdict on *imperialism* as a tool of black liberation." A subhead in Wilt's essay notes, in *Black Panther*, "sole black militant portrayed as completely deranged."[10] Serwer, on the other hand, titled his article "The Tragedy of Erik Killmonger," and if we understand the character as more tragic than deranged, then neither he nor his politics are particularly vilified. Even if we were to grant that he is indeed "completely" deranged, the film *still* doesn't conflate his derangement with his politics. N'Jobu and Nakia both speak in lucid terms against Wakanda's isolation. W'Kabi embraces Killmonger's interventionism but is far from "deranged."

Another writer, Christopher Lebron, really wanted to like *Black Panther* but was disturbed by its "shocking devaluation of black men." "Rather than the enlightened radical" presented in the comics, Killmonger "comes across as the black thug from Oakland hell bent on killing for killing's sake—. . . a receptacle for tropes of inner-city gangsterism."[11] Serwer, though, argues that the movie explicitly holds that Killmonger "is not a product of the ghetto" so much as a product of the "American military-industrial complex."[12]

Killmonger, we see, is many things to many people.

Lebron argues that Killmonger isn't even granted the luxury of the super-villain's eternally promised return; his death seems too final. But Serwer, and I have to agree, sees the permanence of his death as that rare thing for the superhero genre, a death that actually matters: "The pathos of his tragic end cannot be infinitely repeated as farce."[13] Lebron sees in this quiet death, with T'Challa and N'Jadaka sharing a Wakandan sunset, a missed opportunity "for the movie to undo its racist sins":

> T'Challa can be the good person he desires to be. He can understand that Killmonger is in part the product of American racism and T'Chaka's cruelty. T'Challa can realize that Wakanda has been hoarding resources and come to an understanding with Killmonger that justice may require violence, if as a last resort. After all, what else do comic-book heroes do but dispense justice with their armored fists and laser rifles?[14]

Lebron's article is titled "*Black Panther* Is Not the Movie We Deserve," but his issues might lie more with the genre itself. In his book on Black superheroes, Adilifu Nama wisely counsels that "racial justice is an ambivalent and ambiguous topic best used as a point of departure in superhero comics rather than a real time battleground to make definitive declarations concerning black liberation as an integral aspect of American democracy, freedom, and societal improvement."[15]

Those who wanted a blockbuster superhero movie to advocate for Black revolution were always going to be disappointed. Yet the movie's rejection of Wakandan isolation looked refreshingly progressive to many, surprised to find *any* explicit political discourse in a superhero movie. In a strange way, the question of *Wakanda's* responsibility to the world morphed into the question of *Black Panther's* responsibility to the world.

I can't discount the fact that I fall within the parameters of the viewer satisfied with the "white comfort" offered by the movie, even as I understand how its utopian "solution" to the problems of society doesn't go far enough. I'm satisfied in part because I recognize, with Richard Dyer and Stuart Hall, that the purpose of entertainment isn't to solve society's ills. *Black Panther*, like so much popular culture, is messy, and the messiness of its politics manifests in this multiplicity of readings. "Black popular culture, like all popular cultures in the modern world, is bound to be contradictory," writes Hall. "It can never be simplified or explained in terms of the simple binary oppositions that are still habitually used to map it out. . . . No struggle can capture popular culture itself for our side or theirs."[16] Recent Hollywood movies about Black history and politics have tended toward uplifting neatness: *Just*

*Mercy* (Destin Daniel Cretton, 2020), *Marshall* (Reginald Hudlin, 2017), *Fruitvale Station* (Coogler, 2013), *42* (Brian Helgeland, 2013), *Harriet* (Cassie Lemons, 2019), *12 Years a Slave* (Steve McQueen, 2013) and *Selma* (Ava DuVernay, 2014)—worthy films all, but relatively uncomplicated in their sympathies. Strangely, or maybe not so strangely, genre movies have presented baggier, less comfortable visions: consider not just *Black Panther* but also *Get Out* (Jordan Peele, 2017), *Us* (Jordan Peele, 2019), and *Sorry to Bother You* (Boots Riley, 2018). The more time I've spent with *Black Panther*, the longer I've worked with it, the more I marvel at the ways it complicates and unsettles the terms of the conflict at its center.

Such complications are at the heart of some of the best scholarship on the movie. Babb's situating of *Black Panther* within a longer tradition of Black utopian fiction, for example, demonstrates that its central conflicts are practically archetypal and speak to historical debates that far transcend the place of Wakanda in the Marvel Cinematic Universe or the status of Erik Killmonger as a villain.

My own analysis, like these others, will turn on the problem of Erik Killmonger, but by other means, moving beyond the script (what it *says*) to think about *Black Panther* as a movie: an irreducible aesthetic, phenomenological, and rhetorical experience (what it *does*). There's something to be said for good old-fashioned film studies, since movies, like any aesthetic form, aren't just delivery systems for some stable abstraction called "content," be that content the "story" or a "message." After all, as Nicholas Ray famously said (but maybe didn't), "If it's all in the script, why make the movie?"[17]

That means returning to the issue of performance—considering not only how Killmonger and T'Challa are written but how they're acted. The characters in *Black Panther* don't just espouse their ideological positions, they *struggle*, through their lived experiences, to articulate or understand their place in the world, and performance contributes mightily to our awareness of their struggles.

One thing about Killmonger is that he's a difficult man to read. If there is an undecidability or indeterminacy in *Black Panther*, it's vested in Killmonger himself. He confides in no one, and he is more comfortable declaiming his ideological mission than in revealing anything of himself. Such characters are at the center of Christopher Freeburg's *Black Aesthetics and the Interior Life*, briefly introduced in an earlier chapter. Freeburg advocates against confining our understanding of "the horizon of racial conflict and black aesthetics" entirely to the terms of Black collective politics, and he privileges moments of opacity and unknowability that complicate essentialist assumptions and emphasize public existence.[18] In rejecting that confinement, he rejects the singularity of "the" Black experience.

In his posthumously published *The Eloquent Screen*, Gilberto Perez makes the case that film studies needs to be more attentive to the workings of cinematic rhetoric, the medium's strategies of "argument and persuasion, of different points of view that can be taken and different ways of expressing them and influencing others."[19] Just about any narrative movie solicits a viewer's attention, emotions, and/or intellect through representational and nonrepresentational cinematic elements. Some are more explicit about it, some even do it through tactics of alienation, but the goal must be some sort of audience investment.[20] The movies privileged by Perez—many of them

Hollywood studio films—engender complex, even contradictory ideas and feelings, appropriate to his sense that attention to rhetoric is most urgent "in an era," like ours, "that mistrusts certainties and embraces differences."[21] Given the diverse critical responses *Black Panther* has summoned forth, it seems to be just that sort of movie.

Rhetoric is most effective when it moves beyond the "factual" and the invocation of "principles that presumably speak in the same way to everyone everywhere" to speak instead "in the terms of a concrete social situation to the particular human beings living in that situation."[22] We call these particular human beings *characters*; movie audiences respond to characters in situations. Identification, then, is crucial to cinematic rhetoric, and, not to get too far ahead of ourselves, performance is crucial to the establishment of identification. An actor interprets a script (guided in varying degrees by a director), but performance is also somewhat autonomous, not easily reduced to "meaning." As I'll argue, Chadwick Boseman and Michael B. Jordan contribute immeasurably to our sense of, and ideas about, T'Challa and Killmonger—*immeasurably* here used literally, not hyperbolically.

I've already considered a distinction between moral and corporeal identifications in the superhero movie, but "identification" is one of those terms in film studies that has been long used but poorly understood. What Murray Smith calls "the casual scenario of character identification" depends upon the viewer becoming "attached" to a character "on the basis of qualities roughly congruent with those we possess, or wish to possess."[23] In this strongly affective and seemingly passive relationship, we "take" the character's feelings, informed by the narrative context, as our own.

Noël Carroll rejected this model, arguing, "In order to understand a situation . . . we need only have a sense of why the protagonist's response is appropriate or intelligible."[24] Smith calls this an *alignment* rather than an identification. Alignment emerges through *spatial attachment*, the extent to which action is focused through a character, and *subjective access*, the viewer's knowledge of a character's feelings, thoughts, and motives. Some movies align viewers with a single character, but many move them between or among several (and rare is the TV show that doesn't depend on an ensemble cast).[25]

Perez emphasizes that our relationship to characters depends on multiple contexts—story, setting, and genre—but also the context of the movie in the world, and "whatever context we bring to the work."[26] This last is important, for identification is "always partial. . . . You are still you even as you imagine yourself in someone else's place."[27] The most basic structure of cutting between characters in dialogue solicits identification with both of them, though "not necessarily . . . to the same degree or in the same way." Watching a movie, then, "entails a play of identification apt to shift and complicate and multiply."[28]

What Smith calls *allegiance* corresponds to what I earlier called moral identification—an identification with what the person stands for, implicitly or explicitly.[29] One can be aligned with a character but feel little sense of ideological allegiance (Harley Quinn for some; Dirty Harry Callahan for me). Your usual superhero movie would solicit our allegiance in no uncertain terms—they're called super*heroes* after all—even as we might feel some sympathy for or engagement with the villain. Superheroes traditionally exist in unrealistically pure dichotomies with supervillains, but tragic villains with

understandable motives (Killmonger) or corrupt heroes seduced by power (*The Boys*) can complicate things.

There's also the rhetoric of genre—the horizon of expectations that audiences bring to a genre film. The superhero
genre could be understood as generating an implicit rhetoric
of physical power and performance, of the place of the individual within confining social systems, of changing relations
to technology or shifting notions of identity. In this book I've
emphasized the corporeal utopia of the superhero body and
the implications of the intersection of superhero power with
racialized or gendered cinematic bodies, especially in *Black
Panther*.

*Black Panther*, though, is also *explicitly* rhetorical. The
history of Africa; issues of national, diasporal, and personal
identity (and responsibility); and methods of effecting political
change are all investigated by the movie's rhetorical system,
which includes scripted words and genre expectations (which
are followed, revised, or subverted), and—remarkably for a
superhero movie—its plural sites of identification and sympathy. Viewers need to actively negotiate their positions more
than the "casual scenario" of identification would suggest or
allow.

Compare the parallel introductions of Black Panther and
Killmonger. T'Challa is first seen in the Talon Fighter, on his
way to exfiltrate Nakia (and provide some quick superhero
action). The audience is quickly given information about his
identity: the camera is behind him as he watches news coverage of his father's murder, tracking slowly forward before
cutting to a side shot of the Panther mask resting on his lap.
The next shot slides up from his torso to his face in profile.
He, then, must be the "Black Panther" of the movie's title, and,

too, he is the man beneath that mask. It's a minor bit of spatial attachment. Viewers also have subjective access: close-ups present him as grieving and pensive; the weight of his helmet/crown seems to weigh heavily upon him. The news footage efficiently provides backstory and context for his emotional state.

We meet T'Challa unmasked, and indeed movie superheroes spend a lot of time with faces uncovered. In the comics, superheroes used to wear their masks even while just hanging around the Batcave. But as everyone from D. W. Griffith onward has realized, the expressive face in close-up is a fundament of cinematic storytelling and empathetic identification. And audiences like to see the faces of their movie stars (faces, not so incidentally, for which movie studios pay a *lot*). *Iron Man*'s brilliant innovation was to show us Tony Stark (Robert Downey Jr.) inside the mask, his face framed by the various heads-up displays. In *Black Panther*, T'Challa only wears his mask in the brief Nigerian battle, the car chase in Busan, the glorious moment when he returns from his presumed death, and the final extended battle with Killmonger. Killmonger wears the mask he pilfered from the Museum of Great Britain but only once, and briefly. In superhero cinema, as in cinema more generally, faces, not masks, tell the story and engage the audience.

But alignment is a function of extradiegetic elements as well (something Perez doesn't consider). We understand the character to be our hero through the casting of Chadwick Boseman, recognizable either from *Black Panther*'s posters and trailers or from other Boseman movies in which he played characters of great nobility or genius.[30] Some might already know the Black Panther character from comics, where his hero cred is always evident, or from his introduction to the MCU in

*Civil War* (or, belatedly, through his appearances in *Infinity War* and *Endgame*). Through a host of means, viewers become aligned with Black Panther (and we *always* root for the hero).

Erik Stevens, a.k.a. N'Jadaka, a.k.a. Killmonger, is less known at first meeting, but a similar tracking shot at the museum introduces him. This parallelism gives us to understand that these characters are related; perhaps it's a clue to their status as doppelgängers. It at least affirms that this is another major character. It, too, generates spatial attachment. Erik (not Killmonger to us yet, unless you already read the comics) is young, *very* cool, and way less brutal than Ulysses Klaue, his partner in theft. Klaue and his gang do the killing that follows, leaving Erik relatively unsullied despite his theft of an African mask because he is "just feelin' it." He's pretty darn likable, so the audience "feels it" too. His likability is also a function of casting Michael B. Jordan, who generally plays good-hearted kids who can't catch a break—more about that later. Erik is chatty, explaining himself at every turn. Even if *Black Panther* tilts increasingly toward allegiance to T'Challa and his world, the audience continues to have, for over half of the movie, both attachment *and* access to Erik (there's even a good fifteen minutes when T'Challa is absent from the movie altogether). Here, at the outset, his actions may position him as the movie's villain, but his initial, entirely justified, postcolonial anger elicits positive feelings.

Without saying anything about the validity of his politics, it's easy enough to make the case that Erik is the villain of the piece: it's a superhero movie, ergo he's the villain. He engages in to-the-death conflict with the hero, of whom he's a shadow version. With his ascension to the throne, he exhibits a supervillain's megalomania: "The sun will never set on the Wakandan empire," he proclaims from his seat of empire. He kills indiscriminately (including, in an act of particular cruelty, his vivacious girlfriend, who surely must have had a larger role in the movie at some point). He breaks the rules of the challenge, spearing and killing Zuri ("I'll kill you *both*, Uncle James!"). He resembles the archvillains Magneto (liberating "his people") and Loki (a problematic, but not unlikeable, family member). He tries to destroy the heart-shaped herb and is beginning to export hugely powerful vibranium weapons for the purposes of global insurrection. (This was a very easy list to generate.)

On the other hand, he's played by Michael B. Jordan.

No, really.

If there is one single thing that complicates the audience's relation to Erik/Killmonger/N'Jadaka, it's the casting of Ryan Coogler's longtime collaborator in the role. Jordan came to prominence in the first season of *The Wire*, playing Wallace, one of the kids involved in low-level drug dealing in the low-rise projects of Baltimore. Wallace wants out, but after he's coaxed into giving information to the police, he's killed at the hands of two of his friends. Jordan brought to the role an extraordinary sweetness and vulnerability; Wallace's death will forever break our hearts. There's a shyness in Jordan's portrayal that carries through to his other roles. In *Friday Night Lights*, he's a troubled teen given the choice between playing high school football or heading to juvie, but he is pointedly described as a "decent kid." Here, and in the characters he plays in Coogler's movies—Oscar Grant, Adonis Creed, Erik Killmonger—Jordan gives us a character who knows the streets but isn't beaten down by them. Each is, as they sing in

*Hamilton*, young, scrappy, and hungry; life doesn't come easily to any of them. As Creed says, "I been fightin' my whole life. I ain't got a choice," or as Erik says, accusingly, "Y'all sittin' up here comfortable."

The movie also depends upon the casting of Chadwick Boseman, who brings with him the associations of the larger-than-life real-life characters he's previously played. Jordan's characters, including Killmonger, struggle. T'Challa, on the other hand, and Chadwick Boseman? They were born kings.

To fully appreciate the complex relation viewers might have with Killmonger, it's worth looking more closely at where *Black Panther* sits in relation to Coogler's earlier movies as well as Jordan's place in them. Our identification with characters (in all the ways discussed above) is crucial to a movie's rhetorical strategies, and Coogler is masterful at encouraging identification, empathy, and—his word—intimacy, no matter the scale of the project.

Toward the end of the prologue, after Wakanda cloaks itself from the world's view, the camera moves out to reveal the darkness of Africa (which we now know is not so dark). The world turns; the darkness of the Atlantic comes into view as the boy asks, "Do we still hide, Baba?" Glimmers of light appear: the bright cities of the United States. "Yes," answers the father; the child asks why. The score intensifies and the camera's quickening trajectory tracks in to a particular point on the globe—Oakland, California, in the year 1992. The worlds of oral storytelling and myth fade, and a more modern and naturalistic world comes into view. A pickup basketball game is being played outside a housing project, with a milk crate for a hoop and unpainted wood for a backboard.

Ryan Coogler was born in Oakland in 1986. That would make him, oh, about six years old when this action takes place—not quite Erik's age, but close enough. Coogler's mother continues to work as a community organizer there; his father was a juvenile hall probation counselor. The movie will end with T'Challa and Shuri returning to these projects, which will now house a Wakandan outreach center for this disadvantaged community. Coogler's first film, *Locks* (2009), was set in Oakland, as, of course, was his first feature, *Fruitvale Station*. Oakland's presence in *Black Panther* is an early clue to the personal nature of this blockbuster; it's also where the Black Panther Party was founded, in 1966—which is also the same year Black Panther first appeared in comics.

*Black Panther* begins, then, with an elegant entangling of myth with threads of histories that encompass the personal, political, racial, and superheroic. This thickened present thickens still more as the movie cuts from the bluish glow of the Wakandan aircraft above the clouds to the bluish glow of a TV tuned to coverage of the Los Angeles riots. Two Black men, N'Jobu of Wakanda and his partner, James (secretly Zuri of Wakanda), are involved in planning something quite likely to involve the guns on the table.

*Fruitvale Station* is based on the real story of Oakland resident Oscar Grant, shot in the back and killed by a BART police officer while handcuffed, face down, in the early hours of New Year's Day in 2009.[31] The film tracks his final day and has all the virtues of an indie feature: intimate scale, restricted space and time, location shooting, an emphasis on incident over causality, and, but for Octavia Spencer, a talented but not star-laden cast. Coogler was about Oscar's age when the shooting occurred; he has repeatedly noted that what happened to

Oscar could have happened to him or to his friends. The film is humanist by definition—in the wake of Oscar's posthumous vilification (the "he was no choirboy" syndrome), Coogler saw the film as "an opportunity to show he was a human being."[32] White audiences, I suspect, may have been the ones that most needed to learn that particular lesson.

*Fruitvale* is entirely focused through Oscar. Up to the moment of his shooting, we never leave him (in the aftermath, we experience the shock and terror of his partner, his mother, his friends). We're strongly aligned with him spatially and have unique subjective access. Oscar's all-too-human failings are introduced early: the first dialogue is with his child's mother and her concerns about another woman he's been with; a later flashback shows an angry outburst in prison (which will find its echo at the beginning of *Creed*); he also tries to sell some weed. There are, then, some obstacles to Oscar's gaining our allegiance. But we also experience, with him, his distress at losing his job (for being late), his struggle to "get back on [his] feet," the pleasures of his mom's birthday dinner, and an impromptu New Year's party on a delayed train.

From *Locks* through *Black Panther*, Coogler's camera is aligned and allied with his protagonists' movements; it shares their space. In *Fruitvale*, it's with Oscar in his car; it rides an escalator with him; it's on the ground as he's shot. (The birthday dinner takes place in a room so cozy the camera has to stay in the hall.) Somewhere along the way, the viewer steps away from judgment and into an acceptance of Oscar: his generous spirit, his dedication to friends and family, his vulnerability. He has our wholehearted allegiance. By the time of the shooting it's obvious that nothing he's done, *whatever* he's done, whatever he *could* do, could possibly merit a death sentence.

But how viewers ultimately feel about Oscar—the extent of their affective identification with him—exceeds the choices Coogler, as writer and director, and cinematographer Rachel Morrison make, and has much to do with their engagement with the actor on screen. Oscar is Michael B. Jordan's first starring movie role. Coogler created the opportunities for the audience's alignment with Oscar, but it's Jordan's performance that wins its sympathy and allegiance, as it will again in Coogler's second movie, *Creed*.[33] That movie is a reboot of the Rocky franchise. Coogler pitched the story, got Sylvester Stallone on board (who, uncredited, wrote his own scenes), co-wrote the screenplay, and directed. Jordan stars as Adonis Creed, the unacknowledged son of Rocky's respected adversary Apollo Creed, who had died in an ill-advised bout with a Soviet boxer.

We meet "Donnie" first as a parentless boy whose anger and recourse to his fists have landed him at a youth detention center; he doesn't know the identity of his father until he's taken in by Apollo's widow. The movie jumps to the present, where Adonis is fighting amateur bouts in Mexico as "Donnie Johnson." After quitting his day job, Donnie makes his way to Philadelphia, where he enlists the long-retired Rocky Balboa as his trainer. He's unwilling, though, to take on his father's name. Circumstances will demand that what is only his second professional fight will be for the light heavyweight championship, and it *will* be fought under the name Creed.

The differences between these two movies is stark: *Fruitvale Station* had a $900,000 budget; *Creed*, $35 million. Apart from Jordan, then better known for his TV work, Octavia Spencer was the one "name" in Fruitvale; *Creed* boasts Phylicia Rashad, Tessa Thompson, and, of course, Stallone. *Creed* is more expansive and more classically plotted, moving efficiently

from Los Angeles to Philadelphia and toward a championship
bout in Liverpool. It builds to a rousing and triumphant climax
to a triumphal score (by Göransson, also of *Panther*) heavy on
horns and drums. Jordan plays an emergent superstar rather
than an all-too-ordinary young adult.

And yet the similarities overwhelm the differences. Creed,
like Oscar Grant, is somebody's son, with an absent father
and a strong mother. Strong mothers played by strong actors
loom large in Coogler's films: Spencer, Rashad, Bassett. Oscar's father goes unmentioned and unseen, Apollo died without knowing Donnie, and N'Jobu is killed at *Panther*'s start.[34]

Despite the big budget and the genre trappings, *Creed* is
very much a character study—again, humanist from the ground
up. Apart from the impressively shot fight sequences, it's sur-
prisingly quiet, very like *Fruitvale*, with the same naturalistic
pace, improvised dialogue, and comfortable pauses. The camera hugs Donny close, following him, for example, from the
dank Tijuana locker room to the ring where absolutely *nobody*
is in his corner (soon Rocky will be in his corner, along with his
girlfriend, but overall I think Jordan's characters can be fairly
described as *having nobody in their corner*).

Creed, like N'Jadaka/Erik/Killmonger in *Black Panther*, has
many names: Donnie Johnson, "Hollywood" (his ring nick-
name), Adonis Creed. He knows and doesn't know who he is
or what his names mean. Donnie, as a boy wanting to know
about his unknown father, asks, "What was his name?" (the
movie's title, "CREED," appears imposingly upon the screen).
"Howya doin'?" Rocky mumbles. What's ya name?" Later, Donnie reveals his anxiety to Bianca, his girlfriend: "I'm afraid of
taking on the name and losing." "Use the name," she tells him.
"It's yours."

In *Fruitvale* and *Panther*, Jordan plays potential alter-egos to Coogler, who was about the same age as Grant when Grant was shot and killed, about the age of Erik when he's left fatherless. Coogler's father, the juvenile hall probation counselor, probably met lots of Donnies, but more provocative is Coogler's own Creed-like status as somebody whose second gig came with immeasurably higher stakes and visibility than his first.

And Jordan co-starred in Coogler's next movie, *Black Panther*, which could as easily have been called *The Tragedy of Erik Killmonger*, budgeted at $200+ million.[35] *Black Panther* allies us with him from his first moments. The camera closes in on him at the museum; the curator, who belongs here after all, inserts herself into *his* cinematic space. As he moves from artifact to artifact, the camera moves with him, curator in tow. Although Jordan doesn't play the title character (that role had been cast long before), Jordan's presence couldn't help but resonate with his other work, especially that with Coogler. The fundamental gentleness and decency that Jordan brings to Killmonger from his previous roles—and there's a bit of Wallace in all of them—complicates the audience's relation to this ostensible villain. It isn't, though, an instance of casting against type: everything we like about Jordan's characters is there in Erik. He's *still* a decent kid who can't cut a break: Donnie Creed without the surrogate family and the outlet of boxing. It's heartbreaking that he actually finds a surrogate family in the world of Wakanda, but finds them much, much too late.

When all's said and done, *Black Panther*'s lasting greatness as a work of cinema might lie in the convergence of these two star actors and the archetypes they embody.[36] Boseman's characters are confident, graceful, regal, entitled. They're often way out in front, waiting for the world to catch up, while Jordan's are at the world's mercy (or at least start out that way). They're not graceful (Creed is less graceful than powerful), but they are stubborn. A quick comparison of their two "lawyer movies," each based on real people and cases, tells us much about their respective "types." In *Marshall*, the titular lawyer, played by Boseman, is already established and deeply confident, and has seen it all. In *Just Mercy*, Jordan is Bryan Stevenson, founder of the Equal Justice Initiative, when he's just a green lawyer getting the runaround from the white establishment. Speaking of his death-row client, convicted on coerced testimony, Stevenson says, "Coulda been me." But both lawyers win their cases against steep odds.

To consider Killmonger without reflecting on the casting of Jordan and the types he plays, as well as the way he plays the character, is to overlook a fundamental part of the experience of the movie, and the way that identifications shift and complicate and multiply.[37]

But despite what I claimed earlier, casting isn't the only thing that moves the needle on an audience's relation to Killmonger. He takes down the pompous museum curator. He's hella cool. We meet him as a small and helpless boy. He doesn't hail from a hidden land of privilege and safety. His admirable father has been killed and he abandoned by the Wakandan side of the family. He's disrespected by the tribal council and his cousin T'Challa. He's beautiful and articulate, with a winning smile. He makes genuinely good arguments about Wakanda's obligations to the oppressed. He'd rather die than live in bondage. He's the one African American in the movie. When T'Challa/Panther returns, seemingly from the dead, to the field of battle and yells his name, Erik meets his challenge with a small smile and a "Wassup?" Y'gotta love the guy, at least a little .

Killmonger isn't the first colorful villain with a claim on audience sympathy, but his politicized backstory, the unambiguous way he's been wronged by Wakanda, and his postcolonial sensibility establish him as something more than an "interesting" villain. And, again, there's Jordan, who's never entirely convincing as a badass; it's one of his greatest performative strengths. There's a vulnerability and a lingering sweetness beneath the bravado.[38]

We know T'Challa better than Killmonger (but, as we'll see, our alignments and allegiances aren't so straightforward). Unlike Erik, he engages in introspective dialogue and is spoken about by characters who know him well. T'Challa has the explicit support of his family, the tribes, the elders, his departed ancestors, and even, ultimately, M'Baku (who joins the ruling council by movie's end). Because of this, his father's crimes— the murder of N'Jobu and the abandonment of N'Jobu's young son—are something T'Challa can neither believe (at first) nor accept (ever). Zuri, who spied on N'Jobu, tells T'Challa that they covered everything up, including the existence of the child, because they "had to maintain the lie." "The lie" could be that there's an illegitimate, half-American claimant to the throne (which is as I read it); Coogler, however, holds that "the lie" is Wakandan exceptionalism itself, the nation's belief that it's better than any in the "outside" world. If it interacts with that world, as W'Kabi warned, Wakanda will become "just like everywhere."

Exceptionalism, and an accompanying myth of infallibility, also figures, Todd Burroughs argues, into Ta-Nehisi Coates's analyses of Wakanda (in his *Black Panther* comics) and America (in *Between the World and Me*).[39] America sees itself, in Coates's words, as "a lone champion standing between the white city of democracy and the terrorists, despots, barbarians, and other enemies of civilization."[40] In his comics, some of these very despots and barbarians chide T'Challa and his royal lineage: "You see yourselves as heroes uncorrupted by the dirty work required to remain on the throne";[41] "One cannot, at once, claim to be superhuman and then plead mortal error."[42]

While T'Challa lies near death, Ramonda administers the smuggled heart-shaped herb; once more he finds his father on the Ancestral Plane, who tells him that the time has come for him to join his ancestors. But T'Challa has questions. "Why didn't you bring the boy home?" he asks, pleadingly. "Why, Baba?"[43] T'Chaka replies, "He was the truth I chose to omit." He admits no fault, for he is, like Wakanda, infallible. T'Challa's tragic flaw has been his unwavering faith in family and Wakandan tradition, which has kept him from embracing his kinship to N'Jadaka or from recognizing the threat now posed by Killmonger; because of it, he's incapable of forestalling the civil war he provokes.

In a film that constantly plays innovators against traditionalists, T'Challa has been emphatically, and self-admittedly, "old school."[44] But this is his breaking point. "*You were wrong!*" he shouts, condemning not just T'Chaka but all his ancestors, wrong "to turn your backs on the rest of the world. We let the fear of discovery stop us from doing what is right. *No more!*" T'Challa cannot surrender to the placidity of the Ancestral Plane until this "monster of our own making" is dealt with. He has broken with his father, his ancestors, with the traditional view of Wakanda's place in, and responsibility to, the world. T'Challa must return to the world, if only to put Wakanda on a different path.

When they first met in this spiritual realm, T'Chaka told his son, "It is hard for a good man to be king." There is suppressed guilt in T'Chaka and in Zuri; their duties superseded their humanity. T'Challa has come to recognize the folly in this, and, to be the king he wants to be, he must become not just a good man but a *better* man—wiser, more compassionate—than his father.

T'Challa, though, had learned of Killmonger's identity and history well before, when, in his first gesture of rebellion, he forced Zuri to tell him of their crime. Yet in the later scene in the Tribal Council, he keeps that information to himself. When he knows the truth and *still* resists the legitimacy of Killmonger's claim, our allegiance ought to waver, at least a little.

*Y'all sittin' up here comfortable.* Killmonger's arrival in the council chamber marks the first meeting of the two main characters and the actors who play them.[45] And it's telling: Erik is in shackles but belligerent and unbowed; he's about to reveal his Wakandan heritage. But Jordan does what he often does: his weight shifts back and forth in a constant, restless search for balance, for something firm under his feet, while Boseman plays T'Challa as all steel and focus. Coogler staged a similar contrast in *Creed*: as Adonis "Hollywood" Creed faces off against "Pretty" Ricky Conley before the start of the fight, he's all "anxious, awkward energy," bobbing and rocking and shifting.[46] Conley stands stock still, even his eyes unmoving, locked on Creed. Watching *Black Panther* in the context of *Creed*, you realize that this shifting might be something other than a mark of Killmonger's unstable place in the world; it might be a fighter's tactic, a need to stay light on his feet, ready for whatever's coming from whichever direction.

But T'Challa is in control: Boseman has said that he brought some of Thurgood Marshall's gravitas to the scene, and like a good trial lawyer, he doesn't fully tip his hand. He knows who Erik is, but his unwillingness to accept the truth causes him to waver not a jot. This is, as Coogler puts it, his "mortal error."

As the second challenge duel begins, Killmonger paces restlessly, stripping off his shirt to reveal the patterns of his self-inflicted scarification. And there it is: Michael Jordan's body, startling to behold, which had also been displayed to great advantage in *Creed*. He is buff in *Fruitvale*, bulked in *Creed*, and beyond ripped here in *Black Panther*. Boseman's is not the only beautiful Black body on display in this movie, but where T'Challa projects a physical integrity and presence that refuses abjection, Killmonger's body is etched in pain. Each of the dozens of scars that cover his arms and torso represents a kill. But each is also a scar carrying its own hurt, psychic and physical. His body screams abjection but is beautiful nonetheless. Staring down T'Challa, he expresses anger and guilt in equal measure, and the venom in his cadence is slow and stunning: "I *trained*, I *lied*, I *killed*, just to get here. I killed in America, Afghanistan, Iraq. I took life from my own brothers and sisters right here on the continent. And all this death, just so I can kill *you*."

*All this death.*

*     *     *

Following T'Challa's defeat at Warrior Falls, he is presumed dead and is absent from the movie for some fifteen minutes. Much of this time involves the pilgrimage to visit M'Baku of the Jabari Tribe—Nakia, Ramonda, Shuri, and Ross want him to take the herb and replace Killmonger—and the revivification, there, of T'Challa's nearly frozen body. But T'Challa's absence also allows Coogler to align the audience more strongly with Erik/Killmonger/N'Jadaka; and while his megalomania and cruelty become increasingly clear to everyone on and off the screen, his attempt to reach the Ancestral Plane drags us into his trauma and his tragedy.

At the Hall of Kings, the heart-shaped herb is administered, giving N'Jadaka the powers of Black Panther and allowing him access to the Ancestral Plane. No pomp, no ceremony. As did T'Challa before him, Erik re-experiences the death of his father. We return to the aftermath of N'Jobu's killing, all color drained from the scene: Erik and his friends on the basketball court watching the mysterious lights as they move away. He runs to the building. He approaches his apartment door and opens it, the camera following closely. Before him is the apartment—we get the briefest glimpse of something or someone on the floor in back, but there's a quick cut to Erik's slow and stunned reaction, followed by a shot of him cradling his father's body and weeping, an image identical to the one repurposed from *Civil War* in which T'Challa performed the same action for his father.

The attendants shovel the rust-red sands over N'Jadaka's body. He should now ascend to the Ancestral Plane, but instead there he is, walking down the same corridor toward the same door, a man now. With him, we enter the same apartment, the television tuned to a dead channel, a blank spot on the floor where his father had lain. Beyond the window, its vertical blinds like prison bars, sits the Ancestral Plane, just out of reach. N'Jadaka finds the hidden cache in the wall between the Public Enemy poster and that poster of Huey Newton sitting on a rattan throne; he removes his father's leather-bound notebook. He flips the pages, and as he does we see Wakandan writing, his father's gold herringbone chain (later echoed in Killmonger's Panther costume), English writing, a map with the GPS coordinates of Wakanda, and, at the end of the chain, a ring—his birthright.

*N'Jadaka not quite on the Ancestral Plane.*

The page we can read (freeze-frame helps) is a record of N'Jobu's soul-searching. "Who are you?" he asks, wondering at the change in himself. Whether it's the effect of love for his American partner or for his son, he hopes he can help T'Chaka understand how Wakanda might help others who might be strangers but who have the same skin. It turns out that this is more a letter than a journal entry: at the bottom of the page, he writes, "Who are you, my son?" He expresses the hope that his son may know his true name, limned with a bold flourish: "N'Jadaka, son of N'Jobu."[47]

N'Jadaka puts the chain about his neck, and his father's voice is heard: "What did I tell you about going into my things?" We see N'Jobu, with the blurred silhouette of N'Jadaka visible in the foreground.[48] "Hm?" His smile is fatherly, indulgent. "What did you find?" Erik, a boy again but clothed in the adult's hoodie, answers: "Your home." N'Jobu has given him a key—a lip tattoo—in hopes that he might see that home one day. He tells Erik of Wakanda's beautiful sunsets. "But you still may not be welcome. . . . They may say you are lost."

N'Jobu wonders, "No tears for me?" to which Erik—whose tears we've *just seen*—coldly answers, "People die. It's just life around here." Regretful tears fill N'Jobu's eyes: "Well, look what I have done." He is despondent. "I should have taken you back with me a long time ago. Instead we are both abandoned here." Erik, a man now, with a tear-streaked face answers, "Maybe your home is the one that's lost." N'Jobu lowers his head in sorrow, and Killmonger wakens in the Hall of Kings, a caged animal surrounded by strangers, and demands the heart-shaped herb be destroyed. "Burn it *all*!" The script describes him as a new man, "ready to conquer the world," but I think he's ready to destroy Wakanda—if not as a nation, then as an ideal.

*Burn it all!*

The contrast to the serenity and stability of T'Challa's idyll with his own father brutally underscores Erik's isolation and the terrible wrong he's suffered—orphaned and abandoned, the majestic Ancestral Plane where his ancestors dwell only glimpsed through the windows of that same shitty apartment. Rather than a caricature of Black militancy or African American thuggishness, Erik is a man who has been deeply scarred by T'Chaka's, and thus Wakanda's, indifference. Not even N'Jobu, on the Ancestral Plane, understands the depth of his grief. Christopher González sees him as a different archetype: "the black boy whose father has been taken from him through an act of violence." He adds, with a slightly mystified air, "You almost want to root for him."[49]

So, to echo N'Jobu's question, *Who is he?* Is he Erik, the Black boy from the projects raised without family? Erik Stevens, the darling of special ops? N'Jadaka, the abandoned son of Wakanda? The son of N'Jobu, finding a different path for Wakanda? Killmonger, the supervillain nemesis of Black Panther? To me, he's all of them, which is why I've used his various names throughout this book, using whichever one felt most appropriate in the moment. Many of the critics I discussed, though, favored one version over another, which understandably guided their particular understandings of *Black Panther*. But the more relevant question seems to be, Does *he* know who he is?

He *thinks* he's an agent of global Black liberation. He burns the herb and ascends the throne (in a delicious bit of world-turned-upside-down camerawork) a *revolutionary*, and nothing more. In the world of Black Lives Matter, *he's* the one with the power to redress historical wrongs, and that's the way, it seems, we should understand him.

Yet he's also very much an Afropessimist, especially in relation to the shiny Afrofuturism of Wakanda. Does he *really*
believe that vibranium weapons of destruction will bring
about the liberation he claims to want? For Frank Wilderson,
"Afropessimism is premised on a comprehensive and icono-
clastic claim: that Blackness is coterminous with Slaveness:
Blackness is social death: which is to say that there was never
a prior meta-moment of plenitude, never equilibrium, never
a moment of social life."[50] We know nothing of Erik's mother,
he kills his girlfriend without hesitation, and he's been weap-
onized by the US military. His shifting stance makes visible his
lack of equilibrium. He does not live a "social life" and, what's
more, he's out to destroy everyone else's. In their final battle,
T'Challa cautions him that his actions will destroy the world.
Killmonger yells his answer: "The world took everything away
from me!" Wilderson offers some hope that "social death can
be destroyed. But the first step toward the destruction is to
assume one's position (assume, not celebrate or disavow) and
then burn the ship or the plantation, in its past and present incarnations, from the inside out."[51] Killmonger tries to burn all
the heart-shaped herb "from the inside out," but *this* burning
can only lead him further from any sort of social life. Later, as
he sits dying, he refuses treatment: "Just bury me in the ocean,
with my ancestors that jumped from the ships . . . 'cause they
knew death was better than bondage." Death and bondage, the
only alternatives.[52]

Black liberation, then, would be an unreachable goal for
anyone, including Killmonger—something that he will realize, literally at the end of the day under the setting Wakanda
sun. It would be a mistake to take Killmonger at his word.
He isn't just another politicized but misguided bad guy whose

arguments have merit but whose methods "go too far," which is how many critics have read him. (For a by-the-numbers version of this kind of nonsense, see Karli Morgenthau, leader of the "Flag Smashers" in the 2021 Disney+ series *The Falcon and the Winter Soldier*.) He has played the part of the "deranged" revolutionary, out to do what he does "by any means necessary," with no looking back, the world behind him a closed and illegible book. But he's far more interested in burning down the world—the world *that took everything away from him*—than in making it a better place. Ananya Jahanara Kabir contrasts T'Challa's deep hereditary and personal roots with Killmonger's peripatetic rootlessness (she makes the further point that the audience's immersion in the sensory pleasures of Wakanda aligns us with T'Challa all the more—we practically *become* Wakandan).[53]

Erik simply cannot be entirely defined through his politics or his racial identity, even if he thinks he can be. The terror and burn-it-all rage he experiences upon his return to the Hall of Kings smacks, to me, of denial. This is where Jordan's performance is central: he excels at playing characters who aren't as hard as they pretend to be. Coogler and Jordan move viewers between alignment and distance, intimacy and opacity, leaving Killmonger ultimately unknowable.

So Killmonger's commitment to the politics of Black liberation doesn't run as deep as he (or critics) thinks it does. Or maybe it does, who knows? The personal and political are impossible to disentangle in Killmonger; as Dee Marco sees it, his anger reflects his "personal loss and lack of belonging," characteristic feelings he shares with many in the diaspora.[54] There, outside the window, sits an Africa—natural, historical, and spiritual—from which N'Jobu and N'Jadaka are forever removed, engendering both longing and resentment. When we meet Erik, he's standing before a display of African artifacts, but "his relationship to reservoirs of Africanity," Kabir writes, "is mediated by the glass of the museum case."[55] Doreen St. Félix, in an excellent essay, sees Killmonger as "the fly in the [Wakandan] fantasy's ointment," someone whose exclusion refutes its utopian promise: "The mere idea of Wakanda has driven Killmonger completely insane."[56]

Kabir, too, points to an "underlying longing and sorrow at deracination that is the burden of the African American as diasporic subject" but also finds something at stake for those on the *other* side of the Middle Passage.[57] Coogler, she writes, presents "an African American story that constructs the African as initially oblivious to the historical and ethical burden of the transatlantic slave trade, but who must ultimately experience that story, and that burden, as duly shared and *felt*."[58] *Black Panther*, then, is about the education—perhaps even the radicalization—of T'Challa, an education that can only arrive through the pain and rage of Erik/N'Jadaka/Killmonger.

*From the prologue: scenes of the Middle Passage.*

Darieck Scott writes of the ways Blackness has been over-whelmingly figured through the history of Black abjection: a history that comprises enslavement, colonization, lynch-ing, mass incarceration, and so much more is a narrative of "humiliating defeat, a useless history which must be in some way overturned or overcome," but which is too foundational to truly move beyond.[59] Wakanda's utopianism emerges pre-cisely through its having escaped that history; the history of Wakandan Blackness is not one of abjection. But Kabir and Killmonger suggest that its Edenic innocence has come at a high price, a price of which Killmonger is all too aware. He has been torn from Wakanda, his father killed—he is, really, the diaspora writ small. In truth, Wakanda has participated in that history of abjection through its disengagement and in-action throughout modern African history, and more directly in the case of Killmonger; this is what T'Challa and Wakanda must finally acknowledge. Scott asks, "Can blackness-as-abjection be understood or experienced as . . . a resource for the political present—that broadens and even enriches the expanse of what is human being?"[60] Wakanda has no place for Erik, but he has forced the nation to reckon with its own complicity. His abjection will allow the emergence of a more "human" Wakanda that recognizes its duty to a larger world. Utopian, but less naive, less unsullied. Still, though, there's no place for Killmonger.

And so *Black Panther* moves through the tragedy of Kill-monger and the education of T'Challa toward something reparative. The movie is the product, Kabir writes, of an in-tricate dance in which "the African American filmmaker and the assembled African and Afro-diasporic cast confront each other, their collective memories of slavery, and the complex relationship of those on the African continent to those memories."[61] While I've emphasized the way the movie generates sympathy and identification with its major characters, she sees the movie as generating a positive identification with "Africanity" itself. It isn't just T'Challa's or Killmonger's experience we're talking about. As Coogler said in a discussion with other notable Black Panther creators, "I got both these characters living inside me. I think T'Challa and Killmonger live inside of every African American."[62]

The word "beautiful" occurs often in the script for *Black Panther*, but nearly always as scene description, not dialogue. Funny thing: the one who says it the most is Erik. The African artifacts in the museum are "beautiful," as are the sunsets N'Jobu told him about (he's the only other character to use the word). Down in the vibranium mine, just after he's been dealt the fatal blow, through the pain and with tears in his eyes, Erik confesses to T'Challa, "My pops said Wakanda was the most beautiful thing he'd ever seen. He promised he was going to show it to me some day. Can you believe that? Kid from Oakland running around believing in fairy tales." (Recall Coates's suspicion of fairy tales in *Between the World and Me*.) The anger has melted from Erik's face and body, and he suddenly looks so young—like Wallace. T'Challa brings him to the cave entrance near the top of Mount Bashenga; Erik, dying, bathed in the light of the sunset, looks out and simply says, "It's beautiful."

What does it matter how a movie ends? Does narrative "closure" settle and resolve all the dramatic and ideological conflicts that it seems to, or is closure just an illusion pretending to be a resolution? Maybe closure is meant to hide the fact that it's just about time to, as Shuri says at the challenge ceremony, "wrap it up and go home." Killmonger's story "closes" with his dreams of empire thwarted as he bleeds out under the Wakandan sky. Erik Killmonger has been constrained, contained, and punished, his threat neutralized, his beliefs purged, the status quo restored.[63] But our experience of this ending is not as neat as this "closure" would suggest.

Alternating close-ups show us Erik responding to the beauty of what he has finally been able to see—*able to see* because he's finally there but also because he's no longer blind to it—and T'Challa regarding him. The camera comes closer, the shots now over-the-shoulder, bringing us into their shared intimacy. T'Challa searches Erik's visibly suffering face, hurting from wounds both visible and not.

The scene is the movie in miniature, asking viewers to negotiate their relation to the characters (whose relationship is changing) rather than respond to heroes and villains. This fundamental structure—alternating close-ups in conversation—is a privileged form for Perez, because it "entails a play of identification apt to shift and complicate and multiply." It doesn't always work this way, but it does here; we understand them both. "Plural identification," writes Murray Smith, "lies at the heart of the complexity of experience that narrative fiction can offer us." The interplay is strengthened by the richness and irreducibility of performance: Jordan's projection of suffering and regret (not for his actions, but for his life), Boseman's projection of empathy and unexpected responsibility.

The sunset is indeed beautiful, but it also looks a bit artifi-

cial, not unlike the studio-bound dreamscapes of *Black Narcissus* or *Brigadoon*. Vincente Minnelli's adaptation of the
musical *Brigadoon* comes closest in tone to the closed worlds
of his melodramas, and there is something of the family melodrama to *Black Panther*.[64] Fathers and sons, birthrights and
justice—this is some of the same territory mapped in Minnelli's *Home from the Hill* (1960), in which a son confronts his
powerful father about the illegitimate half-brother he knew
nothing about. I think, too, of Rainer Werner Fassbinder's
meditation on the central conflict in Douglas Sirk's *Imitation
of Life* (1959) between an honorable Black woman who's ac-
cepted her subservient status and her light-skinned daughter
who wants to pass for white. What is one's "proper" place?
What choices should Black people make about finding a place
in the world? "The cruelty," Fassbinder mused, "is that we can
understand them both, both are right and no one will be able
to help them." The only option is to "change the world." He
continues, "At this point all of us in the cinema cried. Because
changing the world is so difficult."[65] As for *Black Panther*,
Christopher González suspects that if his "youngest daughter's reaction is any indication, many viewers may have shed
a tear at Killmonger's demise."[66] Shed a tear *with* him, you
mean.

*Creed* ends with Donnie and Rocky climbing that iconic
stairway to the Philadelphia Museum of Art, the one with
the statue of a young Rocky at its top. "It's my favorite place,"
Rocky tells Creed. "You get to the top, you think you can fly."
Rocky has to stop every few steps, catch his breath; Donny
gently shames him: "One step at a time." "Who told you that?"
"Some old guy." When they get to the top, they turn and look

over the city. "Nice view," says Rocky. "You look hard enough, you can see your whole life from up here." These two are friends, family. The scene anticipates the elegiac moment of Erik's death in *Black Panther*—T'Challa and Erik are identically framed: side by side, seen from behind, looking out at that Wakandan sunset. They're family, too, and could have, had their histories played out differently, been friends.

*Wakandan sunset.*

The tone is so far from the triumphalism of most superheroic victories that it scarcely feels like a victory at all. And, as we'll learn, Wakanda will become more prominent on the world stage—Erik has brought about at least some of the change he espoused. Those unanswerable childhood questions—*Do we still hide? Why?*—will be answered, in part through his actions, but now in his absence.

Looking out over the valley, he might be reflecting on the life he could have had but could never have had. There's a tension between the too-beautiful sunset that the movie is presenting to them and to us at that very moment, and our awareness of the exclusion and isolation upon which this Edenic splendor seems to depend.[67] The word "beautiful," spoken only by Erik/N'Jadaka/Killmonger and his father, is tinged with loss and tragedy. It speaks to this place, this dream, from which "Killmonger" is excluded—a dream of peace, a fairy tale from which he has always been forever banned.

# Conclusion

# Why Do We Hide?

There can be no happy resolution to Killmonger's story; he has no place in the world. But with Killmonger, or Erik, purged from the Wakandan utopia, the paralysis of melodrama yields to other genres—superheroes and science fiction—infused precisely with the ability to either change the world or find a new one.[1]

T'Challa takes a knee beside Erik and offers what he can: "Maybe we can still heal you." What I hear is not a statement about the state of Wakandan medicine; we've already witnessed its powers. No, I think T'Challa is wondering more about the possibility of a spiritual healing. But Erik labors under no such illusions. He asks the question with which he began the movie: "Why?" Better to die as his ancestors did, throwing themselves from slave ships, than live in bondage. He pulls the spear from his body and dies. T'Challa stands in respect.[2]

The movie lingers here, and we with it. The voice of Baaba Maal once more sails over the land—the voice, in effect, of Wakanda—as T'Challa again takes a knee. He begins to fold Erik's arms across his body, into the pose that we've learned to associate with the phrase "Wakanda forever."

Everything is as it was, but not. Wakanda will present its true self to the world. M'Baku, representing the self-exiled Jabari Tribe, has become a member of the tribal council. Step Town still looks like the place to be. Nakia and T'Challa are enjoying it once more; he thanks her for saving him and his family. He gives her a tentative kiss, and she looks at him uncertainly. "You can't blame me," he says (Boseman smile). "I almost died." She responds with an enthusiastic kiss of her own (reminding me of Lauren Bacall in *To Have and Have Not*: "It's even better when you help"). He asks her to stay, and she looks as though she might. The camera cranes upward to take in the towers of Birnin Zana, which is followed by a dissolve back to the makeshift basketball hoop in Oakland where the movie began.

The camera moves from the crate to a newer and more professional-looking hoop and follows a new group of kids playing, eventually finding T'Challa and Shuri standing to the side. T'Challa is unmasked; he wears a black outfit with the Panther necklace clearly visible. Shuri is disappointed not to be at Coachella, but T'Challa explains of the adjacent building, "This is where our father killed our uncle."

With a touch of a kimoyo bead, a Talon Fighter above them uncloaks and settles to the ground, subwoofer-y engines pulsing, attracting the kids playing ball. A future student of Afrofuturism shouts, "That's like a Buggati spaceship!" Another chimes in: "Hey, look, we can break it apart and sell it!" A third: "On Ebay!" Shuri trots over to meet them as they cluster about the craft. But one boy, about the same age and build as the young Erik, walks up to T'Challa and asks wonderingly, "Who are you?"

The prologue ended with Erik asking two questions: "Do we still hide?" N'Jobu answers, "Yes." "*Why?*" We never hear the answer but know now that N'Jobu wouldn't have answered convincingly—he no longer believes in hiding. Here at the movie's end (but for some post-credit business), another boy asks another question. "Who are you?" he asks this king, this superhero, who stands before him unmasked and with a smile beginning to peek through.

The answer to the question seems straightforward. T'Challa prepares to answer, but the film cuts to the credits (perhaps tellingly, to "RYAN COOGLER"). Eventually, after a few minutes of Kendrick Lamar and all the stars in motion, the answer appears: "BLACK PANTHER." The credits have answered for T'Challa. Or not. What was he about to say? It might have been his superhero name, but it could also have been his African name. Or his title as an African king. Or his status as a Wakandan, from a country about to take a prominent place on the world stage. There are a lot of possible answers.[3]

Ryan Coogler, in his invaluable director's commentary, notes that "African Americans have had many names over the course of our history. We went from slave to Negro, to African American to Black, you know what I mean?" I return to Freeburg's attention to "ongoing moments where black artists repeatedly invoke and dramatize questions like who am I, what do I value, where do I find community and how the answers to these questions are so often ambiguous, enigmatic, or withheld entirely."[4] One character in the movie has three names—Erik, N'Jadaka, Killmonger—and spends the movie (and his life) trying to find who he is, rather than what he projects. T'Challa has two, and knows who he is, but he learns that some part of him has been protecting a lie. This isn't just a movie about secret identities, it's—more than any superhero movie I know—about the struggle for identity itself.

But that first question, *Why do we hide?*, is about to be answered: *We hide no longer.*

Everything suggests to me that the founding of the Wakandan International Outreach Centers is only the beginning of Wakanda's engagement with the larger world—but it must begin in Oakland. Not only is it the scene of the original crime against N'Jobu and Erik, but it's where, in 1969, the Black Panther Party began its own community social programs, including the Free Breakfast for School Children Program and community health clinics. This is what the Black Panthers meant to Coogler, growing up.[5] But there's an underlying presumption that this is bigger than Oakland: it's now *America* that needs outreach centers. America has become a backwater, "shithole" country in desperate need of some bold NGO intervention.[6] America keeps falling short of its ideals, unable to fix its own systemically entrenched inequities, but perhaps the powerful counter-mythology presented by Wakanda and its Black Panther hero can help the country envision another way.

Loath as I am to admit it, I know that superheroes aren't real. They can't fight real battles—they *are* fairy tales. And, much as some would like them to be, Black superheroes aren't burn-it-down anarchists or revolutionaries out to change the world—they remain superheroes with a superhero's mission: to preserve, not subvert, order. But even if they *never* turn their power against the Man, the oppressor, the "peculiar institution," or the "colonizer," perhaps they represent the potential power to retaliate that James Baldwin called "good enough":

> One needed a handle, a lever, a means of inspiring fear.
> It was absolutely clear the police would whip you and

take you in as long as they could get away with it, and
that everyone else—housewives, taxi drivers, elevator
boys, dishwashers, bartenders, lawyers, judges, doc-
tors, and grocers—would never, by the operation of any
generous feeling, cease to use you as an outlet for their
frustrations and hostilities. Neither civilized reason nor
Christian love would cause any of those people to treat
you as they presumably wanted to be treated; only the
fear of your power to retaliate would cause them to do
that, or seem to do it, which was (and is) good enough.[7]

Black superheroes aren't literally going to save *anyone*, but
that's okay. They only have to *be*—envisioning and embodying the potential of resistance—to articulate the possibility of
change. The utopian power of popular culture doesn't rest on
its ability to fix things; it's "good enough" to imagine a world
in which they're fixed.

I love superheroes for their celebration of bodies that inhabit the world differently, that soar and sail and sometimes
crash. I envy their freedom from Eisenstein's "once and forever allotted form," and the way they proclaim their existence
through flamboyant color and performance. In comics, dispa-
rate artistic styles present these diverse modes of being: the
cosmic visions of Jack Kirby, the graceful postures of Gil Kane's
figures, the emotive force of Neal Adams's melodrama, and the
precision of fashion, gesture, and decor in the work of Joelle
Jones. Live-action movies are comparatively impoverished,
with heroes that look and move too much the same—they're
only human, after all—their colors muted, their powers
interchangeable. But sometimes superheroic joy manages to
break through, often through performance: Chris Hemsworth's

Thor, Brie Larson's Captain Marvel, Margot Robbie's Harley Quinn, Paul Rudd's Ant-Man, all the Spideys in the Spider-verse. Christopher Reeve's Clark Kent/Superman. Boseman's Panther, and the force of his existence, his grace, his music, his beauty.

*From the Boseman-variant Marvel logo on Disney+.*

The outpouring of grief that followed Boseman's death only underscored the impact of *Black Panther*, its utopian dream a gorgeous respite from the intractable problems of the world. *Black Panther* gave us—and continues to give us—a counter-mythology of beautiful, resistant bodies that will not be ignored, erased, or obliterated.

Never underestimate the power of the superhero.

# Appreciations

Are we academics going to look back and find a phenomenon called the "pandemic book"? What will categorize it? I'm not sure, but I do know that the thank-yous for *my* pandemic book need to take a different form. Usually by this point in the process I'd have given a bunch of talks to road test some of the central ideas, or have had more interchange with my colleagues on the office corridor. Professional debts would be cataloged here, and paid. But this was written mostly on my back patio, with some stints outside the skate park while my son Linus scootered (masked, but not in the superhero way), and it was refined and revised in the blessed solitude of my office when some restrictions were finally lifted.

There wouldn't *be* a book had Beth Kessler not taken responsibility for, like, everything else that was going on around us over the past year and a half: feeding us, keeping us safe, and making sure that our son was learning *something* in what our school district called "Virtual Academy." The pandemic ain't over yet, but here we all are, our family strengthened through the addition of Iggy, our pandemic pug puppy. Beth's managerial skills have always been something to behold, but so are her scholarly skills, which got pretty much put on hold for the duration. I'm not proud of how easily I let things fall into the worst kind of systemic gender inequality. This year should be easier for her, thanks more to Pfizer than to me. Beth read very little of the book along the way, but in a million other more important ways made its existence possible.

Ramzi Fawaz, whom I've met, like, four times yet consider a real friend, very gently read me the riot act in a then-anonymous reader's report on a different superhero book proposal, somehow combining respect for my work with a clear-eyed view of its limitations. To whatever extent I've been able to move past those in this book, it's due to my desire to please my "inner Ramzi"; again, no way this could have happened without him.

The mutual admiration thing I have with Donna Kornhaber is fabulous and ongoing, and I'm so happy she invited me to participate in the 21st Century Film Essentials series. She's been engaged every single step of the way, reading, rereading, problem-solving, troubleshooting, and cheerleading. Jim Burr's considered responses and dry humor were a perpetual boon as he helped me navigate the process. Lynne Ferguson helped me with some difficult choices, and Sarah Hudgens's thoughtful and supportive copyediting took everything and made it better—I *love* a good copy editor.

I can't overstate the value of the evaluations and substantial suggestions I received from Donna, and my future best friends Diana Mafe and Samantha Pinto—they've made this book so much stronger it ain't even funny.

My great friend and fellow "Essentialist," the tireless Dana (*The LEGO Movie*) Polan, read this in various drafts, providing equal measures of enthusiasm and pointed critique. Max Suechting made sure I was on the right track early on; those conversations were so good. Linus Bukatman's eye for cinematic (not just automotive) detail served me well on many occasions.

Two years of Superhero Theory students have endured my

testing of these ideas, but I especially have to thank the extraordinary group of grad students I had this spring (2021): Azza Cohen, Alexandra Stiergou, Daniel Akelsrad, Maxwell Mueller, and Connor O'Brien. So smart, so willing to play intellectually, so good humored. I'm so glad I finally got to meet you IRL for beers.

And speaking of drinking, thanks, too, to my virtual pandemic buddies Karin Denson, Shane Denson, and Vivian Sobchack, who kept all things funny and smart, and special shout-outs to our "pandemic pod" of Mary and Alex Nemerov and all the Friday nights on our patio. I'm really sorry about Santa Barbara, but hope that all is forgiven.

# Notes

**PREFACE**

1. Sergei Eisenstein, *Eisenstein on Disney*, trans. Alan Upchurch (Calcutta: Seagull Books, 1986), 5.
2. Not *just* me, but a comparatively small cohort of fans and scholars.
3. Not everyone liked all of these—this is my personal pantheon. The year was prefigured by 2017, which gave us *The Lego Batman Movie* (Chris McKay) and *Thor: Ragnarok* (Taika Waititi).
4. Though if you'll allow me a tiny moment of smug superiority, while I learned a tremendous amount from the Black studies scholars I read, their knowledge of the world of superheroes was sometimes a bit dicey. Not naming names, but among the hilarious scholar bloopers were: Stan Lee as the writer of "Panther's Rage" (it was Don McGregor); Don McGregor as the Panther's first artist in *Fantastic Four* (it was, say it with me, Jack Kirby; McGregor is a writer, not an artist); and starring as Black Panther—drumroll, please—Chadwick Boswell!
5. As Mark Singer put it so pithily, the "Legion of Super-Heroes serves as an example of a comic which espouses platitudes of diversity while actually obscuring any signs of racial difference." Marc Singer, "'Black Skins' and White Masks: Comic Books and the Secret of Race," *African American Review* 36, no. 1 (Spring 2002): 107. Mark Bould addresses similar issues in "The Ships Landed Long Ago: Afrofuturism and Black SF," *Science Fiction Studies* 34, no. 2 (2007): 180.

6. The *Vulture* critic Abraham Riesman has proclaimed the issue as "the moment superhero comics got woke," and I'm not going to disagree. Abraham Riesman, "*Green Lantern* No. 76 Was the Moment Superhero Comics Got Woke," *Vulture*, April 17, 2018, https://www.vulture.com/2018/04/green-lantern -green-arrow-76-woke-superheroes.html.

7. At the trial of the Chicago 7, in 1969, Bobby Seale condemned "this racist administrative government with its Superman notions and comic book politics. We're hip to the fact that Superman never saved no black people." Quoted in Joseph V. Tirella, "Toon Black, Toon Strong," *Vibe*, October 1995, 102–106. Cited in Casey Alt, "Imagining Black Superpower! Marvel Comics' Black Panther." Accessed via the Internet Archive Wayback Machine, https://web.archive.org/web /20110811093147/http://altcasey.com/works/alt_bp.pdf, July 15, 2021.

## INTRODUCTION. TELL ME A STORY

1. *Black Panther*, directed by Ryan Coogler, written by Ryan Coogler and Joe Robert Cole, based on characters created by Stan Lee and Jack Kirby, produced by Kevin Feige (Burbank, CA: Marvel Studios, 2018). A. David Lewis also discusses the implications of this opening request for a story in "The Ancestral Lands of Black Panther and Killmonger Unburied," *Journal of Religion and Film* Vol 22, No. 1, Article 49 (2018).

2. Blair Davis chronicles the brief life of the very first, short-lived, Black superhero in "*All-Negro Comics* and the Birth of Lion Man, the First African American Superhero," *Inks: The Journal of the Comics Studies Society* 3, no. 3 (Fall 2019): 273–297. Coates has wrapped up his run on *Black Panther*, but Marvel will continue bringing in established writers whose reputations were established outside of comics to guide the character. Next up is John Ridley, best known as the screenwriter for *12 Years a Slave* (Steve McQueen, 2013) but more recently a writer of Batman comics.

3. Keith L. Alexander, "Parents of Young *Black Panther* Fans Struggle with Telling Children of Actor's Death," *Washington*

*Post*, August 29, 2020, https://www.washingtonpost.com /local/legal-issues/parents-of-young-black-panther-fans -struggle-with-telling-children-of-actors-death/2020/08/29 /879b7280-ea0e-11ea-97e0-94d2e46e759b_story.html.

4. Carvell Wallace, "Why 'Black Panther' Is a Defining Moment for Black America," *New York Times Magazine*, February 12, 2018, https://www.nytimes.com/2018/02/12/magazine/why -black-panther-is-a-defining-moment-for-black-america.html.

5. It's telling that in the most exciting action scenes in *Black Panther*, the two challenges at Warrior Falls, T'Challa fights without superpowers.

6. Ann Hornaday has lamented the "long line of indie filmmakers who have sprung from festivals to franchises" in recent years. "No sooner do critics and art house dwellers discover an edgy new voice, it seems, than it is immediately co-opted by the great flattening force of Big Comic Book." She's willing to make allowances for Ryan Coogler, but throughout American movie history independent visions have often thrived within the "confines" of studio production. Ann Hornaday, "Comic Books Have Taken Over the Movies. Must They Take Our Indie Auteurs, Too?," *Washington Post*, July 8, 2021.

## THE ROAD TO WAKANDA

1. See my essay "The Boys in the Hoods: A Song of the Urban Superhero" in Scott Bukatman, *Matters of Gravity: Special Effects and Supermen in the 20th Century* (Durham, NC: Duke University Press, 2003), 184–223.

2. Scott Jeffery, *The Posthuman Body in Superhero Comics: Human, Superhuman, Transhuman, Post/Human* (New York: Palgrave Macmillan, 2016), 86.

3. Jeffery, *Posthuman Body*, 151.

4. Richard Dyer, "Entertainment and Utopia," in *Movies and Methods*, vol. 2, ed. Bill Nichols (Berkeley: University of California Press, 1985), 22.

5. Dyer, "Entertainment and Utopia," 28.

6. Leo Braudy, *The World in a Frame: What We See in Films* (Garden City, NJ: Anchor Press, 1976), 155.

7. See "Lost in the Badlands: Radical Imagination and the Enchantments of Mutant Solidarity in *The New Mutants*," in Ramzi Fawaz, *The New Mutants: Superheroes and the Radical Imagination of American Comics* (New York: New York University Press, 2015), 234–268.

8. Dyer, "Entertainment and Utopia," 22.

9. Maurice Merleau-Ponty, *The World of Perception*, trans. Oliver Davis (London: Routledge, 2004), 56.

10. See Scott Bukatman, *Hellboy's World: Comics and Monsters on the Margins* (Berkeley: University of California Press, 2016).

11. Tegan O'Neil, "We Need to Talk about Thanos," *Comics Journal*, June 15, 2018, http://www.tcj.com/we-need-to-talk -about-thanos/.

12. The historical material in this section distills information from Peter Coogan, *Superhero: The Secret Origin of a Genre* (Austin, TX: MonkeyBrain Books, 2006); Bradford W. Wright, *Comic Book Nation: The Transformation of Youth Culture in America* (Baltimore, MD: Johns Hopkins University Press, 2001); and Sean Howe, *Marvel Comics: The Untold Story* (New York: Harper Perennial, 2012).

13. Wright, *Comic Book Nation*, 183–184.

14. Reeve's performance most magically helped us understand why nobody figured out that Clark Kent and Superman were one and the same.

15. See Stephen Prince, *Digital Visual Effects in Cinema: The Seduction of Reality* (New Brunswick, NJ: Rutgers University Press, 2012). For more about the hybridity of the digital superhero, see my "We Are Ant-Man: The Digital Body in a Superhero Comedy," *Journal of Cinema and Media Studies*, forthcoming.

16. Marvel had a few comics, like *Tales of Suspense*, that featured two superheroes, each in their own continuing story.

17. Umberto Eco, "The Myth of Superman," in *Arguing Comics: Literary Masters on a Popular Medium*, ed. Jeet Heer and Kent Worcester (Jackson: University Press of Mississippi, 2004), 156.

18. In this they were like early movie serials. See Scott Higgins, *Matinee Melodrama: Playing with Formula in the Sound Serial* (New Brunswick, NJ: Rutgers University Press, 2016), 39.

19. Richard Reynolds, *Super Heroes: A Modern Mythology* (Jackson: University Press of Mississippi, 1992), 42.

20. Frank Kelleter, "Five Ways of Looking at Seriality," in *Media of Seriality*, ed. Frank Kelleter (Columbus: The Ohio State University Press, 2017), 13.

21. Kelleter, "Five Ways of Looking," 13. He points to a set of "highly engaged readers who regard serial authorship as a delegated office," 19. See also "Serial Pleasures 1907–1938," in Jared Gardner, *Projections: Comics and the History of Twenty-First-Century Storytelling* (Stanford, CA: Stanford University Press, 2012).

22. Stan Lee (w), Jack Kirby (p), and Vince Colletta (i), *The Mighty Thor*, vol. 1, no. 154 (New York: Marvel Comics, July 1968), 18. For activist infiltration, see, for example, Roy Thomas (w), John Buscema (p), and Tom Palmer (i), *The Avengers*, vol. 1, no. 74–75 (New York: Marvel Comics, March–April 1970).

23. Letter from Guy Houghton, *Fantastic Four*, vol. 1, no. 59 (New York: Marvel Comics, February 1967). Cited in Alt, "Imagining Black Superpower!"

24. Stan Lee (w), Jack Kirby (p), and Joe Sinnott (i), "The Black Panther!," *Fantastic Four*, vol. 1, no. 52 (New York: Marvel Comics, July 1966); Stan Lee (w), Jack Kirby (p), and Joe Sinnott (i), "The Way It Began!," *Fantastic Four*, vol. 1, no. 53 (New York: Marvel Comics, August 1966).

25. Directed by Cedric Gibbons.

26. Klaw makes simulated jungle beasts made out of sound; intriguingly, they absorb force and reflect it back, not unlike the Panther costume of the Coates/Stelfreeze run and of the movie.

27. Letter from Henry Clay, *Fantastic Four*, vol. 1, no. 56 (New York: Marvel Comics, November 1966). Cited in Alt, "Imagining Black Superpower!"

28. Fawaz, *New Mutants*, 166.

29. What Adilifu Nama called "'black is beautiful' self-esteem politics." Adilifu Nama, *Super Black: American Pop Culture and Black Superheroes* (Austin: University of Texas Press, 2011), 39.

30. And still later, the Falcon took on the Captain America identity in comics for a time in 2015, and in the Cinematic Universe as of the end of the first season of *The Falcon and the Winter Soldier* (2021).

31. He soon renamed himself Power Man, a name I thought oddly generic in 1974, oblivious to the *Black* Power connotation.

32. NOT von Eeden's best work. For that, see his 1980s series *Thriller*, co-created with writer Robert Loren Fleming.

33. DC revived the Milestone characters in 2021 with some of the original creators and a host of new talent.

34. Quoted in Sean Howe, *Marvel Comics: The Untold Story* (New York: Harper Perennial, 2012), 132.

35. Letter from Gary Frazier, *Jungle Action*, vol. 2, no. 13 (New York: Marvel Comics, January 1975). Cited in Alt, "Imagining Black Superpower!"

36. Letter from Meloney M. H. Crawford, *Jungle Action*, vol. 2, no. 12 (New York: Marvel Comics, November 1974). Cited in Alt, "Imagining Black Superpower!"

37. Letter from Ralph Macchio, in *Jungle Action*, vol. 2, no. 13 (New York: Marvel Comics, January 1975). Cited in Alt, "Imagining Black Superpower!"

38. Peter Bogdanovich, "Interview with Howard Hawks (1962)," in *Howard Hawks: Interviews*, ed. Scott Breivold (Jackson: University Press of Mississippi, 2006), 34.

39. Jonathan W. Gray, "A Conflicted Man: An Interview with Ta-Nehisi Coates about *Black Panther*," *New Republic*, April 4, 2016, https://newrepublic.com/article/132355/conflicted -man-interview-ta-nehisi-coates-black-panther.

40. Wesley Morris and Jenna Wortham, "We Sink Our Claws into 'Black Panther' with Ta-Nehisi Coates," *Still Processing* (podcast), *New York Times*, March 16, 2018, https://www

.nytimes.com/2018/03/16/podcasts/still-processing-we-sink-our-claws-into-black-panther-with-ta-nehisi-coates.html.

41. Morris and Wortham, "We Sink Our Claws."

42. As pointed out by Todd Burroughs, *Marvel's Black Panther: A Comic Book Biography* (New York: Diasporic Africa Press, 2018), 35–36.

43. Ta-Nehisi Coates (w), Chris Sprouse (p), and Karl Story (i), "The World beneath Our Feet," *Black Panther*, vol. 6, no. 6 (New York: Marvel Comics, November 2016), 17.

44. Reginald Hudlin, "The Black Panther: A Historical Overview and a Look to the Future," in *Black Panther: The Complete Collection by Reginald Hudlin*, vol. 1, ed. Mark D. Beazley (New York: Marvel, 2019).

45. Marvel did something similar with Steve Rogers, who was retroactively endowed with powerful heroic tendencies well before he took a super-soldier serum.

46. The beginning of Coates's tenure preceded the release of the *Black Panther* movie, but later issues followed it. It's interesting to see visual ideas from the movie migrate into those comics.

47. Roger Vincent, "Marvel to Make Movies Based on Comic Books," *Los Angeles Times*, September 6, 2005, https://www.latimes.com/archives/la-xpm-2005-sep-06-fi-marvel6-story.html. Equally important to the success of Marvel Studios, though less visible, were Louis D'Esposito (co-president) and Victoria Alonso (head of production).

48. Derek Johnson, "Cinematic Destiny: Marvel Studios and the Trade Stories of Industrial Convergence," *Cinema Journal* 52, no. 1 (Fall 2012): 1–24.

49. Martin Flanagan, Andrew Livingstone, and Mike McKenny, *The Marvel Studios Phenomenon: Inside a Transmedia Universe* (London: Bloomsbury, 2016), 72.

50. Flanagan, Livingstone, and McKenny, *Marvel Studios Phenomenon*, 29. To commemorate what would have been Boseman's forty-fourth birthday, Marvel created a new Boseman/Panther-variant Marvel Studios logo for the Disney+

streaming service (see page 175). "Black Panther | Marvel's New Opening Logo Tribute for Chadwick Boseman," YouTube video, posted November 29, 2020, by JoBlo Movie Trailers, https://www.youtube.com/watch?v=KuBZZCeyk60.

51. Bryan Hitch had modeled his Nick Fury on Samuel L. Jackson for his *Ultimates* comic, which tickled Jackson enough to make him agree to being cast.

52. To be honest, Wikipedia has the whole story, with footnotes and everything, at https://en.wikipedia.org/wiki/Black _Panther_(film). When the BFI began publishing its series of Film Classics books, there was no such resource, and production histories were an important part of the mandate. Times have changed, and between YouTube and Wikipedia there's a lot of information out there.

53. Alice Zhang, "Ava DuVernay Declined Black Panther Because It 'Wasn't Going to Be an Ava DuVernay Film,'" *Vulture*, July 21, 2015, https://www.vulture.com/2015/07/why-ava -duvernay-passed-on-black-panther.html.

54. Lawrence Ware, "The Most Important Decade for Movies about Black Lives," *New York Times*, December 30, 2019.

55. Boris Kit, "*Black Panther* Teaser Trailer Racks Up 89M Views in First 24 Hours," *Hollywood Reporter*, June 12, 2017.

56. Pamela McClintock, "Disney's *Black Panther* Playbook: A Peek at the Marketing of a Phenomenon," *Hollywood Reporter*, February 21, 2018. Channing Hargrove, "Welcome to Wakanda: Fashion for the *Black Panther* Era," Refinery29, February 13, 2018, https://www.refinery29.com /en-us/2018/02/190738/marvel-black-panther-welcome-to -wakanda-collection.

57. Pamela McClintock, "Box-Office Milestone: *Black Panther* Joins Billion-Dollar Club," *Hollywood Reporter*, March 10, 2018.

58. Christopher Campbell, "Every Record Broken by 'Black Panther,'" Fandango, March 21, 2018, https://www.fandango .com/movie-news/every-record-broken-by-black-panther -753009.

59. Bryan Rolli, "*Black Panther* Proves, Yet Again, That
    Diversity Sells in Hollywood," *Forbes*, February 19, 2018.
    He cites the 2017 Hollywood Diversity Report, produced by
    UCLA's Bunche Center for African American Studies, which
    "provided ample evidence that diversity in film and television
    is absolutely profitable when creators prioritize it from square
    one, not by haphazardly employing a few women or people of
    color to flesh out a predominantly white male production."

60. I'm reminded of an *xkcd* comic strip that featured over fifty
    "unprecedented" election situations, each of which was
    overturned immediately: as of 2004 "no Republican without
    combat experience ha[d] beaten someone two inches taller."
    Until George H. W. Bush did. Randall Munroe, "Electoral
    Precedent," *xkcd*, October 17, 2012, https://xkcd.com/1122/.

61. Wallace, "Why 'Black Panther.'"

62. James Wilt, "How *Black Panther* Liberalizes Black Resistance
    for White Comfort," *Canadian Dimension*, February 21, 2018,
    https://canadiandimension.com/articles/view/how-black
    -panther-liberalizes-black-resistance-for-white-comfort.

63. Wallace, "Why 'Black Panther.'"

64. Scott Mendelson, "In *Black Panther*, Wakanda's Women
    Are Both Funny and Fierce," *Forbes*, February 21, 2018,
    https://www.forbes.com/sites/scottmendelson/2018/02/21
    /black-panther-shines-by-letting-wakandas-women-be-both
    -fierce-and-funny/?sh=4303f0f1587b. Tanya Tarr, "How the
    Women of *Black Panther* Teach Us Four Key Leadership
    Styles," *Forbes*, March 27, 2018, https://www.forbes.com/sites
    /tanyatarr/2018/03/27/how-the-women-of-black-panther
    -teach-us-four-key-leadership-styles/?sh=322f1ff546ee.
    Remington Tonar and Ellis Talton, "Wisdom from Wakanda:
    Five Transportation Insights from *Black Panther*," *Forbes*, May
    7, 2018, https://www.forbes.com/sites/ellistalton/2018/05/07
    /wisdom-from-wakanda-five-transportation-insights-from
    -black-panther/?sh=2a19c53a264e. Rolli, "*Black Panther*
    Proves."

65. Alexander, "Parents of Young *Black Panther*."

66. Lindsay Crouse, "Ava DuVernay Isn't Up for an Oscar, but It's Still Her Night," *New York Times*, April 23, 2021.

67. Thanks to Max Suechting for making this comparison.

68. Valerie Babb, "The Past Is Never Past: The Call and Response between Marvel's *Black Panther* and Early Black Speculative Fiction," *African American Review* 53, no. 2 (Summer 2020): 102. A terrific essay.

69. Similarly, Benjamin Dixon: "If the CIA or SHIELD had to be present in the movie for MCU (Marvel Comics Unity) continuity, I prefer my agents as the useless tokens who we all wondered, 'Why is he even here? Why is he speaking?' versus the venerated, authoritative position given in every other MCU movie." "The Most Important Moment in *Black Panther* No One Is Talking About," Progressive Army, February 18, 2018, http://progressivearmy .com/2018/02/18/important-moment-black-panther/.

70. Sitting at the edge of a cliff, bad guy Helmut Zemo tries to kill himself but T'Challa stops him—another echo of the movie to come.

71. He also fits at least part of the template for a supervillain: "a shadow figure of the hero." Terence McSweeney, *The Contemporary Superhero Film: Projections of Power and Identity* (New York: Wallflower Press, 2020), 25.

## BLACK PANTHER'S BLACK BODY

1. Stuart Hall, "What Is This 'Black' in Black Popular Culture?," *Social Justice* 20, no. 1–2 (Spring–Summer 1993): 104.

2. Hall, "Black Popular Culture," 113.

3. Hall, "Black Popular Culture," 108.

4. Cornel West, "The New Cultural Politics of Difference," *October* 53 (Summer 1990): 93.

5. Hall, "Black Popular Culture," 109.

6. Hall, "Black Popular Culture," 109.

7. To be sure, this would constitute only the most limiting, essentialist definition of Black film. Michael Gillespie argues convincingly for a less restrictive (indeed prescriptive) definition, "compelled by disinterest in claiming that the black

lifeworld be the sole line of inquiry that can be made about the idea of black film." Michael Gillespie, *Film Blackness: American Cinema and the Idea of Black Film* (Durham, NC: Duke University Press, 2016), 2.

8. Wallace, "Why 'Black Panther.'" See also my discussion of Black photographic practice later in the chapter.

9. Hall, "Black Popular Culture," 110.

10. Not to mention presumptuous for this white writer.

11. No less an inspiring icon than Michelle Obama tweeted of *Black Panther*, "Young people will finally see superheroes that look like them on the big screen." Michelle Obama, "Congrats to the entire #blackpanther team!" Twitter, February 19, 2018, https://twitter.com/MichelleObama/status /965641575584935936.

12. Frantz Fanon, *Black Skin, White Masks*, trans. Charles Lam Markmann (London: Pluto Press, 1986), 146.

13. The story is *way* more interesting than that. See Jill Lepore, *The Secret History of Wonder Woman* (New York: Alfred A. Knopf, 2014), and Noah Berlatsky, *Wonder Woman: Bondage and Feminism in the Marston/Peter Comics 1941–1948* (New Brunswick, NJ: Rutgers University Press, 2015).

14. See Davis, "*All-Negro Comics*," 289.

15. In *The Falcon and the Winter Soldier* (2021), the resistance to a Black Captain America becomes a plot point.

16. Richard Newby, "*Into the Spider-Verse* and the Importance of a Biracial Spider-Man," *Hollywood Reporter*, December 12, 2018, https://www.hollywoodreporter.com/heat-vision/why -spider-man-spider-verse-is-important-fans-color-1168367.

17. Alexandra Petri, "Sorry, Peter Parker. The Response to the Black Spiderman Shows Why We Need One," *Washington Post*, August 3, 2011, https://www.washingtonpost.com /blogs/compost/post/sorry-peter-parker-the-response-to -the-black-spiderman-shows-why-we-need-one/2011/08/03 /gIQAViObsI_blog.html.

18. Kathleen M. Frank, "Diversify, Rinse, Repeat: The Direct Market, Sales Data, and Marvel Comics' Diversity Cycle," *Journal of Cinema and Media Studies* 60, no. 1 (2020),

153–157. Coates's *Black Panther* actually had a very healthy run, but his excellent offshoot title, *Black Panther and the Crew*, was canceled after only two issues.

19. Ta-Nehisi Coates, *Between the World and Me* (New York: Penguin Random House, 2015).

20. Osvaldo Oyola, "Between the World and Wakanda: Ta-Nehisi Coates and Brian Stelfreeze's *Black Panther*," *Los Angeles Review of Books*, December 27, 2016.

21. James B. Halie III clocks forty-two mentions. "Ta-Nehisi Coates's Phenomenology of the Body," *The Journal of Speculative Philosophy* 31, no. 3 (2017), 495–503.

22. Except perhaps in the Don McGregor Panther sagas, in which the hero's body is continually brutalized—but not because of its color.

23. Coates, *Between the World*, 103.

24. Coates, *Between the World*, 137, 102.

25. Vivian Sobchack not only pointed me to these texts (a few years apart) but also saw the value of considering them together.

26. Fanon, *Black Skin*, 116.

27. Fanon, *Black Skin*, 109. Jean-Paul Sartre, *Being and Nothingness: A Phenomenological Essay on Ontology*, trans. Hazel E. Barnes (New York: Washington Square Press, 1992).

28. Charles Johnson, "Phenomenology and the Black Body," *Michigan Quarterly Review* 32, no. 4 (1981): 606. Charles Johnson was a fabulous polymath, producing essays, fiction (his *Middle Passage* won the 1990 National Book Award), and political cartoons. He even blurbed a volume of Reginald Hudlin's *Black Panther* comics! ("Reginald Hudlin has taken the first black super hero to the mountaintop, where he belongs.")

29. Iris Young, "Throwing Like a Girl: A Phenomenology of Feminine Body Comportment Motility and Spatiality," *Human Studies* 3, no. 2 (1980): 145, 147, 154.

30. *Black Caesar* (Larry Cohen, 1973).

31. Johnson, "Phenomenology and the Black Body," 604.

32. Denny O'Neil (w), Neal Adams (p), and Dick Giordano (i), "Beware My Power," *Green Lantern*, vol. 1, no. 87 (New York: DC Comics, December 1971–January 1972), 7.

33. *It's a Bird*, a comic written by Steven T. Seagle with art by Teddy Christiansen, is the story of a comics writer given the, for him, unwelcome assignment of writing Superman. The book is, in part, a meditation on what "Superman" means. In one section, the writer considers the Kryptonian character as an outsider, and yet: "Suit and The Hat and Glasses / Clark Kent fits right in" more easily than the Black janitor who "doesn't blend in / So much as Vanish in." Steven T. Seagle and Teddy Christiansen, *It's a Bird* (Vertigo Comics, 2004).

34. Paul Laurence Dunbar, "We Wear the Mask," 1895, Poetry Foundation, https://www.poetryfoundation.org/poems/44203/we-wear-the-mask. Accessed July 19, 2021.

35. Burroughs, *Marvel's Black Panther*, 139. Burroughs argues that white writers, including Roy Thomas and Don McGregor, were primarily responsible for this "disempowering," but it doesn't break down quite that neatly. Coates, for example, changed Wakanda into a constitutional monarchy and T'Challa into a figurehead king. That seems pretty disempowering to me. On the other hand, by the end of Coates's run, T'Challa had become, like, the emperor of the universe or something.

36. Dilip Menon writes of the initial comics that there was "from the very beginning a deep ambivalence toward the blackness as much as the African-ness of the Black Panther." "Fifty Shades of Blackness: Recovering an Aesthetics of the Afrifuge," *Cambridge Journal of Postcolonial Literary Inquiry* 7, no. 2 (April 2020): 109.

37. The presence of Boseman's voice, even while he is masked, also serves as a constant reminder of the character's race and provenance—something else cinema offers that comics can't.

38. Alex Szeptycki, in an essay for my Superhero Theory class, Stanford University, Fall 2019.

39. Zakiyyah Iman Jackson, *Becoming Human: Matter and Meaning in an Antiblack World* (New York: New York University Press, 2020), 10. Thanks to Shane Denson for directing me to this wonderful book.

40. Johnson, "Phenomenology and the Black Body," 605. Native Americans were, similarly, historically aligned with the

natural world, either as savages in a savage land or as existing in a more spiritual communion.

41. All quotes from Johnson, "Phenomenology and the Black Body," 605.

42. Jackson, *Becoming Human*, 49. Ava DuVernay's documentary film *13th* (2016) demonstrates how pervasive this language remained throughout the century and beyond.

43. Prefigured, of course, by such pulp heroes as Tarzan of the Apes and the Spider.

44. Davis, *"All-Negro Comics,"* 289.

45. Which is why I can't agree with Jeffrey A. Brown when he writes that "as an African character, Black Panther was aligned with stereotypes of a dark, exotic, and animalistic racial Other." Jeffrey A. Brown, " 'Black Panther': Aspiration, Identification, and Appropriation," in *Comics and Pop Culture: Adaptation from Panel to Frame*, ed. Barry Keith Grant and Scott Henderson (Austin, TX: University of Texas Press, 2019), 300.

46. Jackson, *Becoming Human*, 1.

47. Jackson, *Becoming Human*, 3.

48. Jackson, *Becoming Human*, 35.

49. "The Prosecution: Excerpts from Steve Schleicher's Closing Argument," *Star Tribune*, April 19, 2021, https://www .startribune.com/the-prosecution-excerpts-from-steve -schleicher-s-closing-argument/600047889/.

50. Jeffery, *Posthuman Body*, 141.

51. Jeffery, *Posthuman Body*, 148.

52. Johnson, "Phenomenology and the Black Body," 607.

53. Here's a point deserving of more attention than I'm able to give it: Powerful black men have historically been positioned as threats to white womanhood and white manhood alike, something blaxploitation heroes embodied with verve and something approaching glee. How does Boseman's Black Panther escape the anxiety surrounding powerful Black men and their uncontrolled sexuality? There are a lot of ways to approach this question, but I'll just mention two: the MCU

is by and large a bloodless and sexless universe, in which banter, special effects, and constant revision domesticate and neutralize the threats and consequences of sex and death. And, as in the original comics, one could argue that setting Panther among an entirely Black population sidesteps the issue of Black/white intermingling. I actually don't buy that one in the world of 2021, but it's at least worth mentioning. On the containment of Black male physicality, see chapter 2, "Paul Robeson Crossing Over," of Richard Dyer, *Heavenly Bodies: Film Stars and Society* (London: MacMillan Press, 1986), 64–136.

54. Johnson, "Phenomenology and the Black Body," 600.

55. bell hooks, "In Our Glory: Photography and Black Life," in *Picturing Us: African American Identity in Photography*, ed. Deborah Willis, 42–53 (New York: The New Press, 1996). Specifically, see 45–46.

56. Shawn Michelle Smith, *Photography on the Color Line: W. E. B. Du Bois, Race, and Visual Culture* (Durham, NC: Duke University Press, 2004), 9.

57. Smith, *Photography on the Color Line*, 7.

58. hooks, "In Our Glory," 48.

59. Ben Arogundade, *Black Beauty: A History and a Celebration* (New York: Thunder's Mouth Press, 2000), 8. Cited in Deborah Willis, *Posing Beauty: African American Images from the 1890s to the Present* (New York: W. W. Norton and Co., 2009), xv.

60. Willis, *Posing Beauty*, xxi. The sociologist Maxine Craig has written of the ways that "images of beauty and beauty practices can serve as a focal point for the complex project of racial rearticulation." Maxine Leeds Craig, *Ain't I a Beauty Queen? Black Women, Beauty, and the Politics of Race* (New York: Oxford University Press, 2002). Cited in Willis, *Posing Beauty*, xxxii.

61. hooks, "In Our Glory," 47.

62. hooks, "In Our Glory," 51.

63. Christopher Freeburg, *Black Aesthetics and the Interior Life* (Charlottesville: University of Virginia Press, 2017), 4.

64. Rather than using a made-up language, like Klingon, Coogler opted to connect imaginary Wakanda to historical Africa by using the widely spoken Xhosa language (about 20 million people speak this Niguni Bantu language in South Africa, Nigeria, Lesotho, and elsewhere, as either a first or second language) as the nation's tongue. Xhosa-speaking people had a long history of fighting European colonialism, and the language was also associated with the anti-apartheid movement. John Kani, who played King T'Chaka in *Civil War* and *Black Panther* (where his son played his younger self), is a Xhosa speaker, so it seemed a most appropriate choice. See John Eligon, "Wakanda Is a Fake Country, but the African Language in *Black Panther* Is Real," *New York Times*, February 16, 2018.

65. Reggie Ugwu writes in the *New York Times*, "In a pop taxonomy of black male nobility, he is cut squarely from the mold of Barack Obama—generally cool-blooded, affable, devoted to unglamorous fundamentals," which is largely true but for his James Brown and Levee Green, both of whom blow hot and hotter. Reggie Ugwu, "How Chadwick Boseman Embodies Black Male Dignity," *New York Times*, January 2, 2019, https://www.nytimes.com/2019/01/02/movies /chadwick-boseman-black-panther.html.

66. Richard Brody, "The Lived-In Grace of Chadwick Boseman," *New Yorker*, August 29, 2020, https://www.newyorker.com /culture/the-front-row/the-lived-in-grace-of-chadwick -boseman.

67. Serkis's face is *literally* animated in *The Lord of the Rings* (Peter Jackson, 2001–2003) and *Rise of the Planet of the Apes* (Rupert Wyatt, 2011).

68. Ugwu quotes *42* director Brian Helgeland: "It's the way he carries himself, his stillness—you just have that feeling that you're around a strong person." Ugwu, "How Chadwick Boseman Embodies."

69. Boseman talks about this in a clip from a *20/20* special *Chadwick Boseman: A Tribute for a King*, that aired on ABC on August 30, 2020.

70. I also think of Christopher Reeve, an actor who so perfectly incarnated Superman, that most perfect of heroes, without a mask, and who also died well before his time.

71. Coates, *Between the World*, 130.

72. Coates, *Between the World*, 12, 37, 21.

73. Coates, *Between the World*, 36.

74. Coates, *Between the World*, 70.

75. J. A. Micheline writes:

You can go back and forth on how those folks were depicted and have critiques of that, but they also didn't exist anywhere else. That wasn't a conversation that could be had, say, about primetime television. It couldn't even get to the level of "how are these folks being depicted?" because they just weren't there. For me, in terms of diversity, Marvel was one of the high points.

J. A. Micheline, "Ta-Nehisi Coates on *Black Panther* and Creating a Comic That Reflects the Black Experience," *Vice*, April 4, 2016, https://www.vice.com/en/article/znga8e/ta-nehisi-coates-talks-about-black-panther-and-writing-from-a-black-experience.

76. Jelani Cobb, "'Black Panther' and the Invention of 'Africa,'" *New Yorker*, February 18, 2018, https://www.newyorker.com/news/daily-comment/black-panther-and-the-invention-of-africa.

77. "The Perfect Body," in Jeffery, *Posthuman Body*, 69–92.

78. Archie Goodwin (w), George Tuska (p), and Billy Graham (i), "Mark of the Mace!," *Luke Cage: Hero for Hire*, vol. 1, no. 3 (New York: Marvel Comics, October 1972), 3.

79. This costume idea was imported from the recent comics by Brian Stelfreeze and Coates, though a similarly powered costume shows up in the Icon comic book, worn by Icon's sidekick, Rocket, in 1993. Interestingly, Klaw's sound creatures also reflected force back upon their source.

80. Coogan, *Superhero*, 30–31.

81. Scott Bukatman, "Secret Identity Politics," in *The Contemporary Comic Book Superhero*, ed. Angela Ndalianis (New York: Routledge, 2009).

82. Johnson, "Phenomenology and the Black Body," 608.

83. Johnson, "Phenomenology and the Black Body," 609.

84. Johnson, "Phenomenology and the Black Body," 609.

85. Johnson, "Phenomenology and the Black Body," 610.

## THE WAKANDAN DREAM

1. Until that moment, I hadn't realized how mainstream the concept had become.

2. Mark Dery, "Black to the Future: Interviews with Samuel R. Delany, Greg Tate, and Tricia Rose," in *Flame Wars: The Discourse of Cyberculture*, ed. Mark Dery, 179–222 (Durham, NC: Duke University Press, 1994). Specifically, see page 180.

3. Dery, "Black to the Future," 180. This latter comparison feels a little problematic today, but I know what he means.

4. N. K. Jemisin, "How Long 'til Black Future Month?," September 30, 2013, http://nkjemisin.com/2013/09/how-long-til-black-future-month/.

5. Dery, "Black to the Future," 180.

6. Dery, "Black to the Future," 182.

7. Mark Sinker, "Loving the Alien: In Advance of the Landing," *The Wire*, vol. 96, June 1992. Accessed via the Internet Archive Wayback Machine, http://web.archive.org/web/20060209100352/http://www.thewire.co.uk/archive/essays/black_science_fiction.html, December 27, 2020.

8. Dyer, "Entertainment and Utopia," 222.

9. Hall, "Black Popular Culture," 113.

10. Sinker, "Loving the Alien."

11. Nama, *Super Black*, 39. Also, on the same page: "If ever there was a compelling black superhero that appeared directly drawn from the political moment yet presented an Afrofuturist sensibility, T'Challa, the Black Panther superhero of Marvel comics, is such a character."

12. See "X-Bodies: The Torment of the Mutant Superhero," in Bukatman, *Matters of Gravity*, 48–78.

13. Nama quoted in Chauncey DeVega, "Is 'Black Panther' the First Real 'Black Science Fiction Film?,'" *Salon*,

February 17, 2018, https://www.salon.com/2018/02/16
/is-black-panther-the-first-real-black-science-fiction-film/.

14. In fact, Marvel's Black superheroes will rally to save Wakanda
at the climax of Coates's Intergalactic Empire of Wakanda
saga.

15. Samantha Pinto, "Wakanda and Black Feminist Political
Imagination," *Black Perspectives*, March 24, 2018, https://www
.aaihs.org/wakanda-and-black-feminist-political-imagination/.

16. Wallace, "Why 'Black Panther.'"

17. He relates this in his 1982 concert film, *Richard Pryor: Live
on the Sunset Strip* (directed by Joe Layton). He continues,
"I been here three weeks, I haven't even said it. I haven't
even thought it. And it made me think, 'Oh my god, I been
wrong. I ain't never gonna call another Black man n*****.'" I
struggled as to whether to use the word he uses or eviscerate
his language with ellipses or euphemisms, but I figure if
Pryor decided that word was over, then there you go. The
deeply moving clip can be found at "Richard Pryor the N
Word," YouTube video, posted April 14, 2012, by Kurt Wagner,
https://www.youtube.com/watch?v=hULhZqhw9yU.

18. Pryor can, I think, be forgiven for overlooking the bloody
history of tribal conflict and other messy truths about African
history. To his diasporic eyes, this was a kind of utopia.

19. Steven Thrasher, "There Is Much to Celebrate—and Much to
Question—about Marvel's *Black Panther*," *Esquire*, February
20, 2018, https://www.esquire.com/entertainment/movies
/a18241993/black-panther-review-politics-killmonger/.

20. Lee, Kirby, and Sinnott, "Black Panther!," 4–5.

21. Lee, Kirby, and Sinnott, "Black Panther!," 9.

22. Often posed as a problem, this sort of appropriation is the
mechanism by which cultures replenish themselves and stay
vital. See Ann Douglas, *Terrible Honesty: Mongrel Manhattan
in the 1920s* (New York: Farrar, Straus, Giroux, 1995).

23. Wallace, "Why 'Black Panther.'"

24. Kelleter, "Five Ways of Looking," 16.

25. Kelleter, "Five Ways of Looking," 25.

26. Don McGregor (w), Billy Graham (p), and Klaus Janson (i), "Once You Slay the Dragon," *Jungle Action*, vol. 2, no. 11 (New York: Marvel Comics, September 1974).

27. Don McGregor (w), Billy Graham (p), and Craig Russell (i), "The God Killer," *Jungle Action*, vol. 2, no. 13 (New York: Marvel Comics, January 1975), 17.

28. Christopher Priest (w) and Mark Texeira (p, i), "The Client," *Black Panther*, vol. 3, no. 1 (November 1998). A map of Wakanda in *The Official Handbook of the Marvel Universe* (1983) notes that the "Techno Jungle" is beneath the palace.

29. From the "Page to Screen" featurette on the *Black Panther* Blu-ray release.

30. Dana Polan steered me to this clip and suggested that it would go well with the discussion of Beachler's detailed research. Matt Morrison, "A College Student Gave a Presentation on the Power Struggle in Wakanda—and His Professor Had No Idea It Was a Fictional Nation," *Business Insider*, June 6, 2018, https://www.businessinsider.com/college-student-fools -professor-with-presentation-on-wakanda-2018-6. Video at "Power Struggle in Wakanda," YouTube video, posted June 5, 2018, by DZastr22, https://www.youtube.com /watch?v=WLPJ2kPQD4w.

31. Tonar and Talton, "Wisdom from Wakanda."

32. "Specifically, it was projects like Hadid's DDP Building in Seoul, the MAXXI museum in Rome, and Wangjing SOHO in Beijing that left their mark on Beachler's psyche." Mark Wilson, "Meet the Designer Who Created Black Panther's Wakanda," *Fast Company*, February 23, 2018, https://www .fastcompany.com/90161418/meet-the-designer-who-created -black-panthers-wakanda.

33. The shot is repeated, just as thrillingly, in *Infinity War*, thus proving the point.

34. See "The Artificial Infinite: On Special Effects and the Sublime," in Bukatman, *Matters of Gravity*, 81–110.

35. A clue might be found in Coogler's interview with David Greene on NPR's *Morning Edition* on February 15, 2018: "I think intimacy can be achieved in a film of any budget.... I

have some of my most intimate scenes that I've ever made in this movie."

36. Jemisin, "How Long."

37. Jemisin, "How Long."

38. "Astro-Blackness is an Afrofuturistic concept in which a person's black state of consciousness, released from the confining and crippling slave or colonial mentality, becomes aware of the multitude and varied possibilities and probabilities within the universe." Reynaldo Anderson and Charles E. Jones, "Introduction: The Rise of Astro-Blackness," in *Afrofuturism 2.0: The Rise of Astro-Blackness*, ed. Reynaldo Anderson and Charles E. Jones (Lanham, MD: Lexington Books, 2016), vii. Jemisin contributed to the world of Afrofuturist and Astro-Black superhero comics with her excellent *Far Sector* series, in which a young, Black, queer, and very green Green Lantern tries to quell political tensions on a distant metropolis planet. N. K. Jemisin (w) and Jamal Campbell (a), *Far Sector* (Burbank, CA: DC Comics, 2020–2021), 12 issues.

39. W. E. B. Du Bois, *The Souls of Black Folk* (Oxford: Oxford University Press, 2007), 8. First published 1903.

40. Morris and Wortham, "We Sink Our Claws."

41. We were similarly introduced to T'Challa, an echo to be discussed in the next chapter.

42. Doreen St. Félix: "He looks like a charming blipster." "On Killmonger, the American Villain of 'Black Panther,'" *New Yorker*, February 20, 2018, https://www.newyorker.com/culture/culture-desk/on-killmonger-black-panther-s-american-villain.

43. Coogler discusses this on his commentary track.

44. In the 2019 movie *Harriet* (Kassi Lemons), Tubman chastises her abolitionist allies in similar language: "You've gotten comfortable."

45. Pinto, "Wakanda and Black Feminist."

46. My students raised this question, one likening it to the scene in *Monty Python and the Holy Grail* (Terry Gilliam and Terry Jones, 1975) in which Arthur explains how he became king to a politically progressive peasant, who observes, incredulously,

that "strange women lying on their backs in ponds handing out swords is no basis for a system of government."

47. Another contrast might be the climactic issue of Coates's "Intergalactic Empire of Wakanda" comics storyline, where seemingly every Black superhero converges on Wakanda to protect it from intergalactic-N'Jadaka's assault: a self-evidently justified convergence that needs no explanation.

48. Again, the design of her lab owes something to Ken Adams, set designer for many a James Bond movie.

49. Although there *is* a brief Easter-eggy glimpse of them in more formal wear at the United Nations during the movie's post-credit sequence.

50. Elisabeth Abena Osei notes that powerful women were "commonplace in pre-colonial African communities—throughout West Africa, women were known to have controlled their own worlds, speaking on matters of taxation, and the maintenance of public facilities including markets, roads, wells and streams." "Wakanda Africa Do You See? Reading *Black Panther* as a Decolonial Film through the Lens of the Sankofa Theory," *Critical Studies in Media Communication* 37, no. 4 (2020).

51. Diana Adesola Mafe, *Where No Black Woman Has Gone Before* (Austin: University of Texas Press, 2018), 3.

52. Mafe's book is especially resonant for Okoye, who is, like Zoe in the TV show *Firefly*, a physically intimidating warrior who "simply does not fit" into comfortable female paradigms (*Where No Black Woman*, 129). Like Selena in *28 Days Later*, who would kill the protagonist "in a heartbeat," Okoye answers her husband W'Kabi's question in the battle sequence— "Would you kill me, my love?"—by drawing her weapon: "For Wakanda? Without question." She even appears, like Selena, in "drag"—Selena wears a red dress in her encounter with some unfriendly soldiers, and Okoye is disguised with a red dress and wig at the casino. Mafe writes that Selena "remains a singular face of womanhood that is not easily appropriated or dismissed, especially by a phallocentric white gaze." Mafe, *Where No Black Woman*, 43.

53. Scott Mendelson praised the movie's avoidance of "badass" woman clichés, and its well-cast "tough and opinionated women" who "were also pretty damn funny as well." "In *Black Panther*, Wakanda's Women."

54. Andrew Kleven, *Barbara Stanwyck* (Basingstoke, UK: Palgrave Macmillan, 2013).

55. Mafe says as much when she acknowledges that writers and directors don't solely determine a movie's affect; rather, "each of the black female characters (and the actresses behind the roles) perform the social constructs of race, gender, and class in ways that challenge audiences to rethink entrenched expectations regarding black femininity." *Where No Black Woman*, 8.

56. The script I'm working from isn't the shooting script but the one submitted to the Academy of Motion Picture Arts and Sciences. Still, it's significant that Okoye's smile isn't highlighted.

57. Robyn C. Spencer, "Black Feminist Meditations on the Women of Wakanda," Medium, February 21, 2018, https://medium.com/@robyncspencer/black-feminist-meditations-on-the-women-of-wakanda-5cc79751d9cd.

58. Wesley Morris, "The Superhero Franchise: Where Traditional Movie Stardom Goes to Die," *New York Times*, May 19, 2016.

59. Their marital status is made explicit in a deleted scene.

60. I, on the other hand, had to look it up.

61. Cobb, "'Black Panther' and the Invention."

62. Jonathan W. Gray, "The Liberating Visions of *Black Panther*," *New Republic*, February 13, 2018, https://newrepublic.com/article/147045/liberating-visions-black-panther.

63. Thanks to Linus Bukatman for the car information.

64. Throw Tiffany Haddish into the mix, and we're a step away from *Girl's Trip 2*. See *Girls Trip* (Malcolm D. Lee, 2017).

65. Harley Quinn (especially as incarnated by either Margot Robbie in live action or Kaley Cuoco voicing the animated version) has finally helped me appreciate and understand cosplay: who *wouldn't* want to be Harley?

66. Tolulope Akinwole, "Embodied Masculine Sovereignty, Reimagined Femininity: Implications of a Soyinkaesque

Reading of Ryan Coogler's *Black Panther*," *Cambridge Journal of Postcolonial Literary Inquiry* 7, no. 2 (April 2020): 155.

67. The comics spoiled any kind of feminist affect, though, by presenting her as stereotypically voluptuous and forcing her into painful "brokeback" postures and the tightest of costumes.

68. But she *might*.

69. Akinwole points out that "where T'Challa's women consolidate and complement his strength, Killmonger kills off his own women." "Embodied Masculine Sovereignty," 157. Ananya Jahanara Kabir makes a similar point in "Alegropolis: Wakanda and *Black Panther's* Hall of Mirrors," *Cambridge Journal of Postcolonial Literary Inquiry* 7, no. 2 (April 2020): 129.

70. I've elsewhere argued that superheroes don't wear costumes to fight crime but fight crime so they can wear costumes. The superhero licenses colorful garb for a demographic that has been dissuaded from flamboyant color—straight white males. See Bukatman, "Boys in the Hoods."

71. David Batchelor, *Chromophobia* (London: Reaktion Books, 2000), 22.

72. Michael Taussig, *What Color Is the Sacred?* (Chicago: University of Chicago Press, 2009), 18.

73. Batchelor, *Chromophobia*, 22–23.

74. Goethe, *Theory of Colors* (1810), cited in Batchelor, *Chromophobia*, 112.

75. Powell and Pressburger's chromophilia permeates their other color films, without reference to either savages or children. Famously, *A Matter of Life and Death* (1946) gives its characters a Technicolor life and a black-and-white afterlife.

76. Taussig, *What Color Is the Sacred?*, 9.

77. Batchelor, *Chromophobia*, 71.

78. Of the three Indigenous characters in *Black Narcissus*, only Sabu has brown skin; the other two are played, wonderfully (but more problematically), by British actors May Hallatt and the fabulous Jean Simmons. *Black Panther* doesn't present any of its characters in dark makeup, but many in the cast are not African.

79. "Pontormo's Rainbow," in Dave Hickey, *Air Guitar: Essays on Art and Democracy* (1997), 48. Cited in Batchelor, 79.

80. Taussig, *What Color Is the Sacred?* Much is conveyed through Carter's costumes, which associate specific colors with characters, just as Ludwig Göransson's score uses musical motifs. Nakia and the River Tribe are coded green, Okoye and the Dora Milaje are armored in red, and the Queen Mother, Ramonda, and Shuri are often in white. T'Challa's color is black—the color that contains all the rest.

81. The Ancestral Plane is known as the Djalia in the comics. Taussig notes that a "human physiological component is rarely absent from the contexts in which color is used in ritual." *What Color Is the Sacred?*, 8.

82. Taussig, *What Color Is the Sacred?*, 6.

83. For architecture, see Sam Aston, "Architectural Inspirations of Wakanda," Matechi, April 2018, https://www.matechi.com /architecture-of-wakanda?fbclid=IwAR33ZkdnSyFWD xzvo2jYi_McgU-wOEy_-N7u1CX1NvdXQkiNbW0vMKnEok. For costumes, see Melena Ryzik, "The Afrofuturistic Designs of 'Black Panther,'" *New York Times*, February 23, 2018, https://www.nytimes.com/2018/02/23/movies/black -panther-afrofuturism-costumes-ruth-carter.html. For more on both, see Eleni Roussos, *Art of Marvel Studios:* Black Panther (New York: Marvel Worldwide, 2018).

84. Ainehi Edoro and Bhakti Shringarpure, "Why Is the Cultural Life of *Black Panther* So Derivative?," Africa Is a Country, February 26, 2018, https://africasacountry.com/2018/02 /africa-is-a-country-in-wakanda.

85. Bill Nasson, "*Black Panther* on Its Continent: Prowling, Pouncing, and Parading," *Safundi* 20, no. 1 (2019): 28.

86. Edoro and Shringarpure, "Why Is the Cultural Life."

87. In an article about Beyoncé's extended music video *Black Is King* (Beyoncé Knowles-Carter et al., 2020), Lauren Michele Jackson contrasts Beyoncé's collaborations with African artists, artisans, and performing artists with *Black Panther*-ish Wakandafication, but I'm pressed to find much

of a difference. Jackson, "Beyoncé's Knowing Ethnic Splendor in *Black Is King*," *New Yorker*, August 3, 2020, https://www.newyorker.com/culture/culture-desk/beyonces-knowing-ethnic-splendor-in-black-is-king. For a concurring opinion, see Haddy Jatou, "Beyoncé Is Not Beyond Reproach," Medium, https://haddyjatou.medium.com/beyoncé-is-not-beyond-reproach-22f877ae43ff.

88. Cooper Hood, "Marvel's Black Panther Working Title Revealed," *Screen Rant*, October 18, 2016, https://screenrant.com/black-panther-marvel-working-title-motherland/.

89. Babb, "Past Is Never Past," 97.

90. Babb, "Past Is Never Past," 100.

91. Cobb, "'Black Panther' and the Invention."

92. Cobb, "'Black Panther' and the Invention."

93. This is where Edoro and Shringarpure wind up, too: "To the extent that it aims to express the natal rupture experienced by African-Americans and the perpetual legacy of traumatic uprooting that is brought upon them, *Black Panther* beautifully evokes it." "Why Is the Cultural Life."

94. Pan-Africanists of course abounded with differing ideas of how to achieve this unification, but the commonality of the dream is what concerns me here.

95. Cobb, "'Black Panther' and the Invention."

96. Wallace, "Why 'Black Panther.'"

97. Kabir, "Alegropolis," 133. Another *very* strong essay.

98. Babb, "Past Is Never Past"; Kabir, "Alegropolis," 130.

## THE KILLMONGER PROBLEM

1. Wilt, "How *Black Panther* Liberalizes."

2. As in *Captain America: Civil War*.

3. See, for example, Barbara Yohan, "*Black Panther*: Analysing One of the Great Comic Book Movies of Our Time," *Movie/Dash*, April 12, 2018, https://www.moviedash.com/editorials/574/black-panther-analysing-one-of-the-great-comic-book-movies-of-our-time/.

4. @leslieleeiii, posted February 17, 2018. No longer available on Twitter but widely quoted elsewhere.

5. Slavoj Žižek, "Quasi Duo Fantasias: A Straussian Reading of 'Black Panther,'" *Los Angeles Review of Books*, March 3, 2018, https://lareviewofbooks.org/article/quasi-duo-fantasias-straussian-reading-black-panther/.

6. Prince Shakur, "'Black Panther' Mirrors the Duality of Martin Luther King, Jr. and Malcolm X," *Teen Vogue*, March 10, 2018, https://www.teenvogue.com/story/black-panther-duality-martin-luther-king-jr-malcolm-x.

7. Jerome Maida, "Michael B. Jordan gets his kicks playing the villain in *Black Panther*," *Philly Voice*, February 23, 2018.

8. Babb, "Past Is Never Past," 99. Rachel Gillett, "Black Panther: A Call to Ethiopia," *Black Perspectives*, May 5, 2018, https://www.aaihs.org/black-panther-a-call-to-ethiopia/.

9. In this (and this alone) he is more like a typical supervillain. Serwer compares him to Magneto, who has similar dreams and is "another comic-book character who is a creation of historical trauma—the Holocaust instead of the Middle Passage." Adam Serwer, "The Tragedy of Erik Killmonger," *Atlantic*, February 21, 2018, https://www.theatlantic.com/entertainment/archive/2018/02/black-panther-erik-killmonger/553805/.

10. Wilt, "How *Black Panther* Liberalizes."

11. Christopher Lebron, "'Black Panther' Is Not the Movie We Deserve," *Boston Review*, February 17, 2018, http://bostonreview.net/race/christopher-lebron-black-panther.

12. Serwer, "Tragedy of Erik Killmonger."

13. Serwer, "Tragedy of Erik Killmonger."

14. Lebron, "'Black Panther' Is Not."

15. Nama, *Super Black*, 98.

16. Hall, "Black Popular Culture," 108.

17. Not to mention the equally possibly apocryphal quote from Samuel Goldwyn: "You want to send a message, call Western Union."

18. Freeburg, *Black Aesthetics*, 4.

19. Gilberto Perez, *The Eloquent Screen: A Rhetoric of Film* (Minneapolis: University of Minnesota Press, 2019), xix.

20. This is true for nonnarrative films, too, though such Andy Warhol films as *Empire* (1964) might (*might*) be considered exceptions.

21. Perez, *Eloquent Screen*, xix.

22. Perez, *Eloquent Screen*, 4.

23. Murray Smith, "Altered States: Character and Emotional Response in the Cinema," *Cinema Journal*, vol. 33, no. 4 (1994): 48.

24. Noël Carroll, *The Philosophy of Horror, or Paradoxes of the Heart* (New York: Routledge, 1990), 95–96.

25. Perez distinguishes between *efficient identification* with "a character's agency as a mover of the story," and *affective identification* with a character's emotional states (adding that these two modes aren't mutually exclusive). *Eloquent Screen*, 251.

26. Gilberto Perez, "Toward a Rhetoric of Film: Identification and the Spectator," *Senses of Cinema*, April 2000, http://www.sensesofcinema.com/2000/society-for-cinema-studies-conference-2000/rhetoric2/.

27. Perez, *Eloquent Screen*, 347.

28. Perez, *Eloquent Screen*, xxi, 348.

29. Smith, "Altered States," 41.

30. Following Boseman's death, some viewers might recognize him from tributes and obituaries, a point too sad to put in the main body of the text.

31. *Fruitvale Station* won the Grand Jury Prize and the Audience Awards at the 2013 Sundance Film Festival, and an Un Certain Regard prize at the 2013 Cannes Film Festival. Forest Whitaker, Zuri in *Black Panther*, was an early backer.

32. Discussed by Coogler in *Fruitvale Station: The Story of Oscar Grant*, a featurette accompanying the movie on DVD/Blu-ray.

33. Writing of *Stella Dallas*, Perez writes, "Stella is no type, not as Barbara Stanwyck plays her." *Eloquent Screen*, 242.

34. In this, it summons thoughts of *The Negro Family: The Case for National Action*, otherwise known as the Moynihan Report, from 1965, which ascribed much of the problem of Black economic struggle to absent fathers. Thanks to Samantha Pinto for the connection.

35. I refer here to Serwer, "Tragedy of Erik Killmonger."

36. There was a different kind of convergence earlier in the careers

of both actors, when they each portrayed the same character, Reggie Porter, on the ABC soap opera *All My Children*. Boseman played Porter for one week in 2003 but didn't like the gang member stereotyping; Jordan stepped in and played the role for the next three years. Zack Sharf, "Michael B. Jordan Landed 'All My Children' after Chadwick Boseman Got Fired for Refusing to Play Racial Stereotype," *IndieWire*, January 3, 2019, https://www.indiewire.com/2019/01/chadwick-boseman-fired-all-my-children-racial-stereotype-michael-b-jordan-1202031999/.

37. In his commentary for the movie, Coogler says that he shares Erik's impatience to move, to get it *done*.

38. Jonathan Gray praises the way Jordan "communicates [his] conflicting motivations, tapping into the same angst and longing that lent pathos and an unusual depth" to his earlier roles. Gray, "Liberating Visions."

39. Burroughs, *Marvel's Black Panther*, 145–151.

40. Coates, *Between the World*, 8.

41. Coates, Sprouse, and Story, "World beneath Our Feet," 8.

42. Coates, *Between the World*, 8.

43. This is the second time this question has been asked of a "Baba"—the first was Erik wondering why Wakanda still hid from the world.

44. See, or rather hear, Coogler's commentary track to the movie for more on the innovator/traditionalist dualities.

45. A brief moment in Korea doesn't really count—they're in separate shots and distant from one another.

46. Bilge Ebiri, "*Just Mercy* Is a Precise and Patient Recounting of a Very Real Human Story," *Vulture*, December 25, 2019, https://www.vulture.com/2019/12/just-mercy-movie-review-michael-b-jordan-and-jamie-foxx.html.

47. This page, so briefly on-screen but accessible to anyone with a pause button, is kind of the Rosetta Stone to understanding Killmonger, whether or not he understands himself.

48. It's never entirely clear whether it's the adult or the child Erik that we see. It seems to be the child, but the ambiguity is important.

49. Christopher González, "A Metonym for the Marginalized," *Safundi* 20, no. 1 (2019): 15, 16.

50. Frank B. Wilderson, *Afropessimism* (New York: Liveright Publishing Corporation, 2020), 102. Priscilla Layne gave a talk on the connection between Killmonger and Afropessimism, which she generously shared with me: "The Marvel of *Black Panther*," Center for African Studies, University of North Carolina-Chapel Hill, March 26, 2018.

51. Wilderson, *Afropessimism*, 103.

52. Coates, discussing the movie with Wesley Morris and Jenna Wortham, describes this moment, his voice rising: "And we're seeing this . . . *in a Marvel Comics movie?*" Morris and Wortham, "We Sink Our Claws."

53. Kabir, "Alegropolis," 11.

54. Derilene (Dee) Marco, "Vibing with Blackness: Critical Considerations of *Black Panther* and Exceptional Black Positionings," *Arts* 7, no. 4 (2018), https://www.mdpi.com /2076-0752/7/4/85. Accessed December 27, 2020.

55. Kabir, "Alegropolis," 128. She further points out that this scene of alienation directly follows T'Challa's return to his home and the glories of Wakanda.

56. St. Félix, "On Killmonger." This is a fabulous piece that I wish I'd written. Actually, the *New Yorker* writers Jelani Cobb, Anthony Lane, and Richard Brody all did very well by *Black Panther*.

57. Kabir, "Alegropolis," 130.

58. Kabir, "Alegropolis," 124.

59. Darieck Scott, *Extravagant Abjection: Blackness, Power, and Sexuality in the African American Literary Imagination* (New York: New York University Press, 2010), 5, 4.

60. Scott, *Extravagant Abjection*, 6.

61. Kabir, "Alegropolis," 121.

62 "Page to Screen" featurette.

63. For Laura Mulvey, containment, punishment, and death are the three "solutions" to unruly women in Hollywood narrative. Laura Mulvey, "Visual Pleasure and Narrative

Cinema," in *Film Theory and Criticism: Introductory Readings*, ed. Leo Braudy and Marshall Cohen, 833–844 (New York: Oxford University Press, 1999).

64. For more on the relation between Minnelli's musicals and his melodramas, see Thomas Elsaesser, "Vincente Minnelli," in *Vincente Minnelli: The Art of Entertainment*, ed. Joe McElhaney, 79–96 (Detroit: Wayne State University Press, 2009).

65. Rainer Werner Fassbinder, "Six Films by Douglas Sirk," *New Left Review* 1, no. 91 (May–June 1975): 96.

66. González, "Metonym for the Marginalized," 16.

67. It reminds me of the death of Sheriff Colin Baker, played by Slim Pickens in *Pat Garret and Billy the Kid* (Sam Peckinpah, 1973). One of the most beautiful deaths in all of cinema.

## CONCLUSION. WHY DO WE HIDE?

1. The rhetorics of two genres collide.

2. This idea partly came from Boseman: "In early drafts of the script, Erik Killmonger's character would ask T'Challa to be buried in Wakanda. Chad challenged that and asked, 'What if Killmonger asked to be buried somewhere else?' Coogler recalled." Rachel McRady, "'Black Panther' Director Ryan Coogler Reveals Chadwick Boseman Inspired One of the Film's Iconic Lines," *ET*, September 1, 2020, https://www.etonline .com/black-panther-director-ryan-coogler-reveals-chadwick -boseman-inspired-one-of-the-films-iconic-lines.

3. I lied: there's another question. In the first post-credit sequence, an elegant T'Challa addresses the United Nations office in Vienna (where T'Chaka was killed). "For the first time in our history we will be sharing our knowledge and resources with the outside world. Wakanda will no longer watch from the shadows." An ambassador cuts in: "With all due respect, King T'Challa, what can a nation of farmers offer to the rest of the world?" Murmurs around the room. Close-ups of Okoye, Nakia, Ross, and, finally, T'Challa, as they share a secret smile.

4. Freeburg, *Black Aesthetics*, 4.

5. Radio interview, *Ebro in the Morning*, February 2018. "Ryan Coogler Breaks Down the Making of 'Black Panther,' Black Girl Power, and Building Wakanda," YouTube video, posted February 14, 2018, by Hot 97, https://www.youtube.com/watch?v=fRpunguFOq4.

6. Thanks to Max Suechting for this insight.

7. James Baldwin, *The Fire Next Time* (London: Michael Joseph, 1963), 32.

# Index

Note: Page numbers in *italics* refer to images.